The NEW Rules

*The dating
dos and don'ts for
the digital generation*

Ellen Fein & Sherrie Schneider

piatkus

PIATKUS

First published in the United States in 2013 as *Not Your Mother's Rules*
by Grand Central Publishing
First published in Great Britain in 2013 by Piatkus
Reprinted 2013 (five times), 2014

A CIP catalogue record for this book
is available from the British Library.

ISBN 978-0-7499-5724-7

Printed and bound in Great Britain by
Clays Ltd, St Ives plc

Papers used by Piatkus are from well-managed forests
and other responsible sources.

MIX
Paper from
responsible sources
FSC® C104740

Piatkus
An imprint of

Little, Brown Book Group
100 Victoria Embankment
London EC4Y 0DY

An Hachette UK Company
www.hachette.co.uk

www.piatkus.co.uk

Contents

Contents

Contents

Acknowledgments

THANKS TO OUR wonderful husbands, Lance and Roger, who were incredibly supportive while we were writing this book, as well as when our office phones rang off the hook with emergency consultations that sometimes interrupted family occasions! And thanks to our fantastic kids, Jason, Jenny, and Rebecca, who gave us their take on texting, Facebook, BlackBerry Messenger, iPhones, Skype, and Twitter! We couldn't have written this book without you...or without our friends who freely shared their time and dating stories!

A special thanks to all our *Rules* contacts worldwide, as well as our dating coaches and clients and fans, who encouraged us to write a new book for the Y generation.

And a drumroll, please, for our brilliant literary agent and friend, Caryn Karmatz Rudy, who was always generous with her time and talent and loyalty for the last fifteen-plus years—and without whom *The New Rules* would have been an idea instead of a reality. Last but not least, thanks to Hachette Book Group USA (formerly Warner Books, which published our first book) and a special shout-out to our visionary editor Amanda Englander, who gave us fabulous direction and guidance and was one of our biggest cheerleaders.

The NEW Rules

Chapter I

Why We Wrote This Book

HAS YOUR MOTHER or another relative, friend, or acquaintance ever said, "You're so pretty, smart, and nice—why don't you have a boyfriend?" Did you feel speechless because you couldn't figure it out either and were not sure what you were doing wrong in the dating department?

Women today manage to graduate with honors, climb the corporate ladder, win Olympic gold medals, and even run for president of the United States, but getting a guy to ask them out or commit is next to impossible! Alas, we know the reason why most pretty, smart, and nice women don't have a significant other: they either pursue guys or act too eager when guys make the first move!

Here's how it all started: About twenty years ago we were having dinner with five friends at a Chinese restaurant on the Upper East Side in New York City, a scene sort of like one from *Sex and the City*, but before *Sex and the City* existed. Every woman brought her dating problem to the table. We noticed that the women who played hard to get, either on purpose or because they were truly busy, got the guys, while the women who asked guys out or showed too much interest got dumped. We put two and two together, watched it work in real life, and decided to write a dating book to share the secrets of this phenomenon to help every woman on earth—not just our friends—date successfully.

Simply put, *The Rules* are a way of acting around any guy who initiates conversation with you, whether in person or online, so he becomes obsessed with you and wants to commit. Yes, it's about playing hard to get, because guys love a challenge and lose interest when anything is too easy—*especially* women.

The Rules became an instant best seller and was translated into twenty-seven languages—because guys are the same all over the world! We appeared on just about every TV and radio show, preaching the play-hard-to-get gospel. We started a worldwide phone and e-mail consultation business and a free *Rules* network; we have helped thousands of women date with boundaries to find self-esteem, love, and marriage.

Now we want to help *you* date successfully; we want to share our time-tested secrets with you, which are applicable whether you're dealing with texting, Facebook, instant messages, or Skype. You can truly do *The Rules* on any guy, in any situation, and get the fabulous payoff: a guy who is crazy about you!

Are you tired of guys texting you or friending or messaging you on Facebook, but not asking you out?

Have you heard of *The Rules*, but are not sure how to apply these dating secrets to today's technologies?

Have you had it with casual relationships and hookups and spending Saturday nights or Valentine's Day alone?

Do you wonder why some women who are not even as pretty or smart or nice as you get the guys, and you don't?

Do you suspect that you are doing something wrong, but are not sure what?

If you answered yes to any of the above, then you are reading the right dating book! We wrote *The New Rules* because how to get and keep a guy is not taught in high school, college, or even later in life. Women both young and old, including our clients, contacts, dating coaches, and those who are getting back into the dating game, begged us to write another book covering the latest shape dating has taken on. Even mothers wrote to us asking how they could help their daughters!

We wrote *The New Rules* to teach women how to capture the heart of Mr. Right in the *new* world of dating and romance. But the truth is, all the old *Rules* still apply! We strongly encourage you to read or at least browse through *All the Rules* in addition to this book; some of the content may seem a bit outdated, but the spirit of our message is still the same. Today there are lots of nuances to the older *Rules* that weren't even on their way to existing yet in 1995! We've included a few *Rules* here that have come up in our previous books, but with updates pertaining to today's dating world. We even use some of the same terminology in this book, like buyer beware (*Rule #22*) and Next! (*Rule #31*). We also wrote a quick reference guide about the most important *Rules* to keep in mind from those books in *20 Rules That Bear Repeating*. Your mother may have bought you a copy of this book, or maybe you bought it yourself to find answers. No matter how it got into your hands, we will teach you how to use *The Rules* in a world full of texting, tweeting, wall writing, booty calling, and more—all of which has changed the way *everyone* dates.

But before you can do *The New Rules*, you have to

understand that men and women are different. This fact may seem shocking because you were raised to think that men and women are equal and that women can do anything they want. Women can become doctors and lawyers and make the same salaries as men. They can run marathons and even run for political office! While all this is true, women cannot be the pursuer in a romantic relationship without the possibility of getting rejected, hurt, or perhaps even devastated. Men and women are not the same romantically. Men love a challenge, while women love security. Men love to buy and sell companies as well as extreme sports like mountain climbing and bungee jumping, while women love to talk about their dates and watch romantic comedies. In fact, one of the guys we interviewed for this book said, "I could never be a girl—you talk about relationships too much!" It's true: A woman gets a text or e-mail from a guy she likes and she forwards it to five girlfriends to analyze it. A guy gets a text, thinks about it for less than a second, and then turns back to the football game. *Vive la différence!*

The other thing you need to understand is that men are extremely visual and cannot be attracted to a girl just because she is nice, smart, or funny. They know who they like instantaneously. It may sound bad, but physical attraction is everything for a guy. He can't possibly love your insides if he doesn't love your outsides, so it's a waste of time to initiate contact. You may not be his type or look and he will eventually dump you for the girl he is physically attracted to. Conversely, while women also have a type/look, they can grow to like a guy who is funny or successful. But a guy just can't do it! Women are more emotional about love and can be swept away by a guy's personality, while most guys can't get past a woman's looks. Yet another way men and women are wired differently!

Knowing these differences between the sexes will help you do *The Rules*—play hard to get—because being a challenge is the secret to getting a guy. Men are easily bored, so if you want a guy to pursue you, don't act so interested. Treat him a little bit like a guy you don't care for! As we wrote in our first book, don't speak to a man first, don't ask him out, don't accept last-minute dates, don't see him too often, and don't date him forever. These are the keys to dating!

So why *The New Rules*—and why now? Facebook, instant messaging, texting, and other social technologies have made it almost impossible for women to be elusive and mysterious. Every woman is glued to her cell phone and guys can reach her morning, noon, and night. Not exactly hard to get! How exactly can a woman do *The Rules* under these new circumstances, you ask?

We were talking to a new client who was just out of college and she was complaining about how hard it is to follow *The Rules* with the new levels of accessibility. She said that, thanks to *The Rules*, she knew not to call men or ask them out. And thanks to *The Rules* for online dating, she got that she shouldn't contact a guy after looking at his profile or respond to a wink. But texting, Facebook, instant messaging, Twitter, and Skype were throwing her for a loop. She didn't know if *The Rules* applied—and if they did, how exactly? She had so many questions! Was it okay to text a guy first? If you had to wait to text back, how long was *Rules*-y and how long was just rude? Were there new *Rules* for all this? With all due respect, she said, technology has changed so much since our previous books were published—everyone texts constantly now and thinks nothing of friending guys and tweeting all day long, so how was it going to all work out for a *Rules* Girl like her?

Another client called with similar questions, and then another client and another, and then our own daughters and their friends were asking us questions, so we knew we had to address these issues—we knew we had to write this book! Everything is different now, and more instantaneous, so how could *The Rules* possibly apply?

We remember back in 1995 when readers labeling themselves feminists scoffed at the idea of not calling men and rarely returning their calls. Now not calling men first is considered normal!

While this book is for a new generation, nothing has changed about what women want in a relationship: to be able to trust that a guy loves them for who they are, and to know that he will be there for them. *The Rules* still apply!

We finally decided to write this book when Heather, twenty-six, e-mailed us about what she thought was a life-altering dating experience. Heather had met a really cute guy at an upscale bar the night before. The next day he had texted her three times before 5 p.m. We were impressed. Three times? "Yeah, I lost my phone. By the time I found it after work the next day, there were three texts from him. The first message was 'hey, it's Cory from last night, great meeting you, text me back when you get a chance.' The second was 'are you doing anything tonight?' And the third said, 'are you free this weekend?' I can't believe I got asked out on a date this soon, I guess he really likes me!"

We told Heather to text him back that night, "Hey, nice

meeting you too. This weekend is great." She did not *have to* divulge that she lost her phone. This way Cory would think that she had other things going on besides him, so he could get used to having to pin her down. Once you text a new guy back immediately, he begins to expect it all the time and the thrill of the chase is gone.

Had she not lost her phone, Heather and Cory would probably have texted back and forth all day and he might have gotten bored and not have been so quick to ask her out. But not having instant access was a breath of fresh air and made him act fast. Heather got to know right away how this guy felt instead of *wondering* how he felt, and also wondering why all the marathon text chatting wasn't leading to a date! What *The New Rules* can do for you is similar to the effect of losing your phone for a few hours here and there. It will help you create an air of mystery and a rare longing from guys.

We also felt compelled to write this book because many of the women who used *The Rules* to get married almost twenty years ago want to see their friends, sisters, and nieces in healthy relationships, or at least not getting hurt unnecessarily by men. They want other women to experience the same happiness they themselves found by dating with self-esteem and boundaries. Older women who are divorced and now back in the dating game or women who have never been in a *Rules* relationship often call us to say how confused they are about e-mailing, texting, and other technology, so we wrote this book to help them as well.

Remember, *The Rules* are an ageless, timeless recipe for romantic relationships. Follow *The Rules* and you get a guy who is crazy about you. Break *The Rules* and you get heartache. Whether you are eighteen or twenty-eight or forty-eight years old, we believe all the answers to your dating dilemmas can be found in this book. Not sure how to act or how to dress on dates? See *Rule #1* and *Rule #2* about being and looking like a Creature Unlike Any Other. Not sure when and how to text a guy back? See *Rule #6*, with our tried-and-true reply timetable. Not sure about splitting the bill or how long to Skype or what to write on a guy's wall? See our chapters on not buying his love (*Rule #19*), long-distance relationships (*Rule #15*), and Facebook (*Rule #10*). We've covered it all! We've also included special commentary from our daughters, who grew up with *The Rules* and can help you apply them to a younger generation and the latest technology. Sometimes a twentysomething can best understand what another twentysomething is going through. We felt it was essential that our daughters weigh in with their unique perspective on the dating dilemmas facing their age group.

If you want to get the full benefit of this book, don't just read it—read it over and over again. Study it like a textbook. You might even want to highlight sentences that help you remember each *Rule*. You might want to meet up with other *Rules*-minded girlfriends on a regular basis to discuss the book and go over your dating problems and our answers as a group—there is strength in numbers! You might want to tear out key pages to put in your bag so you can quickly glance at them in the bathroom on dates.

Without further ado, we present *The New Rules!*

Chapter II

Our Daughters Weigh
In on *The Rules*

As the daughters of the authors of *The Rules*, we wanted to add a little of our own observations and experience in applying *The Rules* to new times and advancing technology. After all, it only makes sense to include our opinions in a book meant, at least in part, to help people in our generation! Obviously, we are not the relationship experts, but we have learned what dating should be like by watching our moms give women everywhere these successful tools for dating. We've heard about every issue you can imagine and how our moms recommended handling them—by now, we pretty much have *The Rules* ingrained as part of our DNA! For us, *The Rules* is not a game you play to catch a guy, but a way of life.

Would we be *Rules* Girls if our mothers *hadn't* written the book? Totally! Our moms have never pushed this way of dating on us, but we both have traditional values and believe in old-fashioned courtship, even today. Guys should always pursue girls first—because it works. The fact that our moms wrote *The Rules* makes us more knowledgeable about the subject, but that's about it. We have seen for ourselves that girls in real life—and on TV or in movies—who chase guys don't feel good about themselves and usually end up getting hurt or dumped.

We have grown up with texting, Facebook, FaceTime, Skype, instant messaging, Twitter, and a whole bunch of other social networking sites. We know that all this instant communication has made dating harder and more confusing. However, we have watched girls make grave errors with guys by writing all over their Facebook walls, tweeting at them, texting them 24/7—we've even seen a few stage 5 clingers, which we promise never ends well.

We all know what it's like to have a huge crush or fall hard for a guy, and not be able to get him off your mind. Obviously that's why all anyone talks about is dating! Invest your time and get busy with work, friends, hobbies, sports, and clubs—not just with guys. Do something you can be proud of for yourself.

The sooner you start learning and doing *The Rules*, the better. We have seen far too many dating heartaches and wouldn't want any of that happening to you!

Chapter III

Do Whatever You Want Until You Are Ready to Do *The Rules*

- Are you okay when a guy you hook up with never texts you again?

- Do you think being asked out last minute is fun and spontaneous, as opposed to insulting?

- Do you ask guys to hang out and just shrug when they say no?

- Do you continue dating a guy who says he is "not looking for anything serious" and who sees other women?

- When your mother or friends suggest *The Rules*, do you say, "I have an MBA. No one is going to tell me what to do"?

IF YOU ANSWERED yes to any of these questions, then keep doing what you are doing. This book may not be for you—or at least not yet. All we can say is, have fun breaking *The Rules* while it lasts. Stalk a guy, write on his wall every day, fly to his city, text him at 2 a.m., and tell him how much you like him. Have the time of your life. Be bold, outrageous, and sassy. Act crazy and carefree!

Let's face it: Most college girls don't want any rules, much less dating *Rules*. They want to do whatever they feel like. They are not thinking ring, wedding, marriage, and children, so why should they give up short-term fun for long-term anything? They may not even have any future plans yet. At this point in their lives, they just want to study and party and hopefully graduate! They want to experiment with sex and possibly with drinking and drugs. They are not looking for anything serious. They want to be silly and flirt with whoever catches their eye instead of waiting for the guy who notices *them* first and makes the first move. They are not looking for husband material. They want the option of going on booty calls when their hormones are raging. They want to run with their feelings instead of being discreet. Why follow a boring set of *Rules* when you are young and have the rest of your life to do that? Why not have fun now and figure things out later?

We totally get it! *The Rules* are simply not for women who just want to have fun. They are for women who get hurt and depressed when a relationship doesn't work out. They are for women who call their best friends, therapists, psychics, or us when they don't know how to get a guy to commit. They do not find random hookups fulfilling anymore. They want a loving, lasting relationship. If you don't feel this way yet, then definitely burn the candle at both ends: text guys all night or hop on a plane to meet an online guy you just friended on Facebook or whose profile you just clicked on.

We frequently get e-mails and Facebook messages from women who feel their sister or friend could really use *The Rules*. They write, "She took back a guy who cheated on her.

She really needs *The Rules*!" or "She's thirty and has been dating this guy for six years and he still hasn't proposed. She needs to wrap it up already" or "My coworker is in love with a married man with kids and I don't think he is leaving his wife anytime soon and I can't get through to her. I wish she would do your *Rules*." Or we get e-mails from worried mothers saying, "My daughter is always chasing guys and getting hurt. I'm worried about her getting a reputation. Can you help her?" We get e-mails from women reading gossip blogs or tabloid magazines who write, "I can't believe so-and-so actress visited him on every movie set and moved in with him. No wonder he thought she was clingy and dumped her. She needs *The Rules*!" We even have *Rules* fans on Facebook who feel that the book should be handed out at birth or at puberty or at least taught in sex education in high school!

Of course, we understand how they feel. It's frustrating to watch a friend or family member or a beloved actress screw up her love life when there is a better way to date. But we tell them what we are telling you here: *The Rules* are for women who want them, not for women who need them. Playing hard to get and dating with boundaries and self-esteem are not easy to do, and no one is going to do it until they have been burned badly and hit rock bottom.

When women buy our book or get in touch with us for consultations, it's not because they arbitrarily woke up one day and decided, "I think I want to be a *Rules* Girl." It's not because they have nothing better to do! It's because they just got hurt by yet another guy in yet another going-nowhere relationship, and desperately want to change their MO. They have endured years of pain and suffering and humiliation, and this last relationship is the final straw. The boyfriend cheated again or the guy they dated for five years never proposed or the married man didn't leave his wife, and they just can't take it anymore! They're tired of waiting or stalking or having fantasy relationships. They're tired of instant gratification with nothing to show for it. They're tired of being dateless to their cousin's wedding. They're tired of being dumped.

In some cases, a woman will contact us because she just met Mr. Right and doesn't want to blow it. After years of breaking *Rules* and settling for random hookups, she finally meets a cute guy and after one kiss she has an aha! moment. She realizes that she does want a healthy loving relationship, not just a lot of texting and sex. She doesn't want to mess it up by coming on too strong ("What are you doing tonight? I have two tickets to a concert") or being needy ("When will I see you again?"). She thinks, "Whoa, I don't want to lose this guy. I need a plan!" When a woman is at this point, when she wants to stop her self-destructive dating habits, she is ready for *The Rules*.

Naturally, we understand that some younger girls reading this book might have a hard time following it. They are in an environment where their friends have frat guys on speed dial and everyone is getting drunk and going on booty calls—not ending dates first! They are still figuring things out and finding themselves. Try to tell your typical college sophomore to have "one drink" and to "wait until she is in a committed relationship to have sex" or "rarely write on a guy's wall," and see how far you get. We have spoken at colleges and at seminars where young women have complained that it's hard to do *The Rules* when everyone they know is texting guys nonstop and hooking up. But the truth is that you can still be a *Rules* Girl regardless of your circumstances or environment. You may not want to get married at nineteen, but you might want to be in a loving relationship in which the guy is crazy about you. *The Rules* give you the upper hand. You have control. You don't get hurt. Now, wouldn't that be nice?

College girls are not the only rebellious ones. We hear from women in their twenties who are into self-discovery and following their hearts—not into thinking hard and abiding by a boring set of dating dos and don'ts. They feel that *The Rules* are not fun or that they are not ready to do them now—maybe in five years. We get it. We also have clients in their thirties, forties, and fifties who are just out of a long relationship or an unhappy marriage. They have not been on a date with a new guy in years. They call us to find out what *The Rules* answer is to their situation, but then they are not ready to follow through. They crave recklessness. They want to act like adolescents and have three-hour textfests and eight-hour first dates and even a few one-night stands.

We had one client who was determined to "sow her wild oats" after being married to a workaholic husband who never wanted sex. After e-mailing a cute guy she met online, she decided to instant message him at 2 a.m. and thought it would be "an adventure" to drive an hour away to meet him at his place that weekend. They slept together and she stayed with him for three days. She said she didn't care if she never heard from him again because she just wanted to have fun and make up for lost time. She heard from him sporadically over a period of three months—only when he wanted her to drive to his place. There were no romantic dinners or loving e-mails. After he ended the relationship by text, she was crushed. She realized that even when you tell yourself, "It's okay if it's just sex," it usually isn't; women want more! So now she is doing *The Rules* and loving it!

We have some intellectual-type clients who argue that

The Rules are disingenuous. They want to "write their own rules" and "let their spirit move them" to e-mail or text a guy or sleep with him. We tell them that this philosophy sounds good, but to call us after they get hurt and/or meet the guy they really want to settle down with. And they usually do! Sometimes they do *The Rules* by accident because they didn't really think they liked the guy and call us triumphantly to say, "I didn't do *The Rules*, and we're engaged." But we explain that just because it was by accident doesn't mean it's not *The Rules*. It's kind of like losing ten pounds without really trying, because you had a stomach flu.

No matter what your age, whether you are a single college freshman or a divorced forty-five-year-old, *The Rules* are for you if you are tired of making mistakes with men and getting hurt or dumped. *The Rules* are for you if want to be in a healthy, loving relationship with a boyfriend and/or future husband, as opposed to one-night stands and instant-message marathons. So when doing "whatever you want" stops working, you'll think about doing *The Rules*! Until then, go wild!

Be a Creature Unlike Any Other

WHEN WOMEN CONTACT us for a consultation, they are usually not feeling great about themselves. The guy they've had a crush on hasn't asked them out, their boyfriend of three years hasn't proposed, or their college sweetheart just broke up with them by text. They feel hurt and inadequate and unlovable. Some want to swear off dating indefinitely or until they feel they can trust men again. They get a pet or eat ice cream, or miss work for days. But we help them get back into the game and reassure them that, regardless of their situation, they are a Creature Unlike Any Other—any man would be lucky to date them! We give them their confidence back.

Being a Creature Unlike Any Other is not about being the prettiest or most popular girl, but about confidence and self-esteem no matter what else is going on in your life. It's about dating with dignity and not being desperate. A CUAO is not anxious or jealous or negative or cynical. She believes in love, even after a bad breakup. She would never say that there's no one good at a singles event or that only losers are on dating websites or that she'll never meet anyone. Instead, she walks into a club like she owns the place and tells herself as she circles the room, "I'm beautiful. Who wouldn't want to talk to me? There is someone out there for me." Of course, she may not really feel this way or totally believe it, but she acts as if she does! If any of us had waited until we felt like dating after a bad breakup, we might *still* be waiting. How long should you wait to date again? One day is more than enough—the best way to get over a guy is just to meet another one! You can cry over your ex while Googling speed-dating events. You have no time to waste!

Being a CUAO is also about doing the best with what you have, not wishing you were someone else. It doesn't matter if you were not popular in high school, if your family is dysfunctional, or if you are unemployed; you are optimistic and don't complain (at least not on dates!). You still show up with a hot outfit and a smile on your face. You hold your head up high without staring at any man; you walk around the room repeating the mantra that you are beautiful and any man would be lucky to meet you! Women are notorious for putting themselves down, so we tell them to pump themselves up. When you are thinking like a CUAO, you are less likely to talk to a man first, go out with him on a moment's notice, or get drunk and then sleep with him.

Alexa, a thirty-two-year-old MBA, called us crying after her boyfriend of three years walked out. She was up all night reading *The Rules* and hysterical after finding out that she had broken every single one of them. We reminded her that she is a Creature Unlike Any Other and that any man would be lucky to meet her. We had her send us some photos and answer some questions so we could create an online profile for her—not the next day or the next week, but that very day. Alexa had modeled during college, so we gave her the user name SmartEx-Model32. She received dozens of adoring e-mails from men in the first few weeks. Well, what man wouldn't want to date a model, former or not? She is now married to a tall, handsome architect on whom she did *The Rules*!

Now, some women argue that calling yourself "Smart Ex-Model" or "PrettyMBA" in an online ad is slightly arrogant or conceited. Aren't we supposed to be more modest? Absolutely not! If *you* don't think you're amazing, who will? Women, especially those who've had their hearts broken, tend to feel like "damaged goods," even if they are pretty and accomplished, so we build them up online!

Another client, Morgan, a forty-year-old accountant, was crushed when the guy she was seeing for six months told her he had met someone else. When she called us, we told her to go to a singles event so that men could drool over her. One guy she met said, "You are gorgeous! Do you have a boyfriend?" Being open and honest, she said, "No, the guy I was dating just broke up with me." Of course, that was not a CUAO response, and the guy ended the conversation abruptly without asking for her number. He probably thought it was TMI. When Morgan called us the next day for a consultation, we said, "You are a CUAO! Why would you tell a guy you were dumped?" The next time a guy asked if she had a boyfriend, she said, "I guess I just haven't met the right one." She is now dating a handsome financial planner.

Being a CUAO means you don't have to answer every question thrown at you. So if you are twenty years old and a virgin and a guy you just met asks you if you've ever had sex, just say, "I'm not comfortable talking about that now." And if you're forty and single and a guy asks why you've never been married, don't say defensively, "I've been engaged twice," just be light and breezy and say, "I just haven't met the right guy yet."

A CUAO would never put herself down or act self-destructively, even if she feels like a failure in the man department. She is not a doormat—she loves herself! She doesn't cave in to peer pressure, nor does she pressure guys to sleep with her or be with her. She's not an open book—she doesn't blab on dates or overshare on Twitter; she listens more than she talks. She's not jealous or mean-spirited, so she would never put down her ex-boyfriend to a new guy or write hurtful things on his Facebook wall. A CUAO would also never sleep with her best friend's boyfriend or have a catfight with another girl over a guy. She believes what's hers is hers!

A CUAO has too much self-esteem to chase guys. She instinctively knows that every guy has a type/look, so whoever likes her will go after her. A CUAO is cool and patient. She waits for guys to make the first move at work, class, a party, or online. She knows deep down that a guy will either notice her or not, so she doesn't try to make anything happen.

A CUAO doesn't rationalize non-*Rules* behavior, online or off. A CUAO is a cyberspace CUAO, too! She wouldn't answer a last-minute e-mail or text that said, "What are you doing in five minutes?" She's busy. She's also not sarcastic or bad tempered. She would never write back in anger, "Not spending it with you!" or lecture men with "Why didn't you ask me sooner?" She wouldn't write back at all, to avoid a flurry of exchanges about nothingness. She hits the ignore button if it's a waste of her time.

A CUAO doesn't try too hard or sweat any situation. She is okay with herself, even if she just lost a job or a guy didn't call her. Instead of eating a box of cookies or getting drunk to drown her sorrows, she gets a manicure and pedicure and goes to a speed-dating party or updates her online dating profile.

When in a relationship, a CUAO doesn't act possessive. She doesn't hang all over her guy in public. She lets him put his arm around her. She lets the guy be the pursuer; she doesn't take that away from him. She lets him take the relationship to the next level, since she appreciates that he likes to make the first move in every way. She knows to let him catch her!

A CUAO isn't needy. She gets attention by *not* trying to get attention. She doesn't have to be loud or overly funny or super witty. She knows that just being in the room or being online is enough. Now that we've explained what a CUAO's inner beauty is, let's talk about how a CUAO should look, as men are visual and must feel a physical spark in order to pursue a woman.

Look Like a Creature Unlike Any Other

IT MAY BE difficult to hear, but we would be lying if we said inner beauty is all that matters. As we have mentioned, most men are obsessed with looks. In other words, most men will not find out how wonderful you are on the inside if they don't like your outsides. Men have a type. Heartthrob actor Leonardo DiCaprio has a weakness for tall, willowy blondes like Blake Lively, Bar Refaeli, and Gisele Bundchen. New York Yankees third baseman Alex Rodriguez favors cute blondes with killer bodies like Kate Hudson, Cameron Diaz, and Torrie Wilson. Dallas Cowboys quarterback Tony Romo also has a thing for beautiful blondes, having dated singers Carrie Underwood and Jessica Simpson before tying the knot with former Miss Missouri Candice Crawford. Tycoon Donald Trump likes tall, gorgeous, European-model types like first wife Ivana and current wife Melania. The point? It's a waste of time to chase guys. You may not be their look, so no matter how wonderful you are, they won't be interested.

Rules consultations include an assessment of a client's looks, both for dates/events and for online dating website profile photos. Here are some general beauty guidelines we suggest:

Hair

Length and Style

Most men prefer long, straight hair—below shoulder length. One of our personal hair stylists who worked at a top salon in New York City and has very high-profile clients did a survey of the men whose hair she cuts. *All* said they loved long, straight hair on women. It's simply the most feminine! Anything above the neck or chin tends to be masculine-looking. We tell clients to grow their hair long or even to get hair extensions. Some women argue, saying that their hair is too thin to wear long or that it's more work to wash and dry long hair. Our answer is, just try it! Others argue that hair extensions are too expensive, but we remind them that they had no problem dropping $500 on airfare to fly to visit their last boyfriend. See how you look! Also, curly dos can look messy, while long, stick-straight hair looks more like one of those luscious shampoo ads. We tell women with naturally curly waves to blow their hair out straight or use hair straighteners.

Color

We often tell women who feel blah with brown hair to try highlights or to go blond. A lighter shade really seems to perk them up. Premature gray hair should be colored immediately, as nothing makes you look or feel older than being silver! Hair is one of the first features a man notices about a woman and should not be ignored or skimped on!

Makeup

Makeup can be tricky for some women. Either they look pale and unfinished or, conversely, they wear too much and look flashy. Neither is flattering. We tell most of our clients to go to the makeup counter of their favorite brand at a local department store and ask for a day look and a night look, as well as instructions on how to re-create both themselves. While many women have their own personal style, we feel that makeup must-haves for a CUAO are bronzer, eyeliner, mascara, and a light-colored lip gloss. This stunning look makes a guy's attention go to the eyes and cheekbones. A tan or bronzer makes you look like you just got back from St. Barts! After the makeover, we tell them to have photos taken to use in their online profiles.

Plastic Surgery

Much has been written on this topic, pro and con, and our feeling is it is up to each woman to decide for herself. While we certainly don't advocate unwarranted surgery, we believe it is important for a woman to feel confident about her looks, and acknowledge that this sometimes requires more than makeup. If a client wants to alter her appearance to feel prettier and more self-assured, we support her decision.

I'm Just Going to College. Do I Really Need to Be a CUAO Today?

We all have days when we'd rather just ditch our skinny jeans and makeup for sweatpants and a messy bun, and we definitely don't see anything wrong with showing up to a morning class looking a little less than our best. We are human, after all. However, if we know a guy we like is in our history lecture, we'll probably throw some eyeliner on that day, but there's no need for over-the-top style to impress your crush during class—we don't want to look like we're trying too hard. On the social scene, though, you can't choose frump over fashion. Having "the look" that gets you noticed isn't so much about which stores you shop at or what brands you wear; it's about showing off your style in a way that demonstrates you've made an effort without being too extreme. You shouldn't meet a guy for lunch wearing an old T-shirt you got years ago; opt instead for cute tops that show off your body, and spend some quality time in front of the mirror. You can experiment with different outfit ideas, but the basic idea is always the same: look like you care and show him that you're beautiful inside *and* out.

—*Rules Daughters*

Other Beauty Essentials

If you have a lot of facial hair—a unibrow or even a mustache—you should get it lightened or waxed. If you have weak nails or bite them, get a gel French manicure that can last two to three weeks. Long nails will make you feel like a goddess, and so will long eyelashes. You may want to have eyelashes put on. Get your teeth whitened, especially if they are yellow or stained from coffee or cigarettes. Wear contact lenses (try blue and green shades!) instead of glasses. Yes, being a CUAO is work. But as Mae West famously said, "There are no ugly women, only lazy ones!"

Clothing

Some women can run corporations or marathons, but they don't have the faintest idea how to dress for men. If a woman wants to catch a man's attention, she should wear sexy, trendy (though not necessarily expensive) clothes, like tops that show some cleavage with a push-up bra and short skirt—anything above the knee. We remind women to dress for men, *not* for other women. Men don't care for flat shoes, even if they are Chanel or Tory Burch; they want you to look feminine in heels, as high as you can stand!

We understand you may have a unique style and we respect that, but in terms of dressing for dating, we feel that a certain look—or uniform, if you will—works best: tops that show some skin, short skirts or tight skinny jeans, and heels. Trouser suits and long, flowing scarves that cover up your cleavage are great for business or having lunch with the ladies, but for guys, you have to look hot, hot, hot! Not slutty—sexy!

Kristi, a thirty-year-old pharmacist, contacted us after her two-year relationship ended with her boyfriend not proposing. In addition to going over all *The Rules* she broke, we went over her clothes, too. She sported a preppy look: crewneck T-shirts and button-down shirts with knee-length skirts and flats. Her hair was pulled back in either a ponytail or a bun. Everything she wore was expensive but boring. She looked like she was going to the library! If she was going to date again, she needed to look hot. We showed her black V-neck, scoop neck, and halter tops, white denim and black spandex skirts, and four-inch-heeled sandals from her favorite store. She had photographs taken after her makeover and shopping spree that actually made her look like a model— she couldn't believe the difference! She is now dating several men she met online and at speed-dating events, and one of them invited her to his sister's wedding. She already knows what she'll be wearing: a short gold sequin tank dress with her four-inch heels. We rest our case!

Experts say you should go through your closet every two years and give away or throw out any clothes that are not sexy or in style. We agree! The same way you should quickly move on from a relationship that's not working is the way you should say good-bye to boring or old clothes, shoes, and bags. Many clients have asked us to help them clean out their closets during makeover consultations—a CUAO does not hang on to frumpy clothes! No one has ever looked back.

Accessories

Again, women have their own personal style. But we think that any *Rules* Girl's best accessory is big (three-inch) hoop earrings in silver or gold. It's a youthful look with long, straight hair and the right makeup. Little or big diamond studs (real or fake) are great when you are engaged or married, but they are too dainty and suburban-looking when you are single. To catch a man's attention you need big, dangling earrings, not ones that get lost in your hair. Big hoops scream *Vavoom!*

Another great accessory is a chunky gold watch. It's bold, modern, and reeks of self-confidence. In fact, a big watch and hoop earrings are about all you need to look hot! Let a man buy you a necklace or bracelet—and eventually a diamond ring. These two simple accessories may sound trendy, but they're not. We've been telling our clients to wear them for the last twenty years—they're tried and true. Brands may come and go, but this sophisticated look hasn't changed. Don't ask, because we can't explain it; we just know it works.

Big sunglasses and the au courant bag are also smart investments. Men may not know Payless from Prada, but they will notice if you are wearing a popular sunglass frame or a cool handbag. So go online or pick up magazines like *InStyle* or *Vogue* and copy whatever celebrities are wearing, but do so within your budget. Wearing narrow or aviator frames when the style is oversized Jackie O or Victoria Beckham–type sunglasses will make you seem out of touch. Similarly, if slouchy, oversized bags are in, you should not be wearing a small bag.

Men want to feel like they are dating a model or celebrity, so look like one!

Rule #3 _____

Don't Talk to or Text a Guy First

IN OUR FIRST book, we told you not to speak to guys first—not even an innocent "Hi" or "What time is it?" Doing so not only shows interest, but goes against the natural order of dating: the guy pursuing the girl. If you speak to or text a guy first, that's making the first move, so how will you ever know if he would have reached out on his own? You won't— and that's the problem!

The intention behind talking to or texting a guy first falls into three basic categories. The first and worst is to create a relationship. The second and more subtle is to remind him that you exist, or even ask him out, if you don't hear from him after a date. The third is to get closure because you haven't heard from him in a while. All three are pretexts for making things happen or keeping a relationship going, and totally against *The Rules*.

Talking to or texting a guy first may make you feel cool, but essentially you're just getting in the back door, creating a relationship that may never have happened otherwise. He may date you because he is flattered or bored or because you're nice, but he probably isn't truly crazy about you. You might get mixed messages from him—sometimes he acts interested, sometimes he forgets you exist—but that isn't a *Rules* relationship. When a guy talks to you or texts you first, he is never ambivalent. He is always interested and always in touch. If you talk to or text a guy first and end up in a relationship with him, you might be confused when he eventually ends it, but trust us, it's because you made the first move.

In a *Rules* relationship, a guy contacts you after a date to ask you out again. You never need to text him first at any point, because he is always texting you about the next date. So if you don't hear from him again, the relationship is over and contacting him to keep it going ("Had a great time, thanks for dinner!" or "Haven't heard from you, is everything okay?") is a ruse that won't work. Your tactics might extend the relationship briefly, but eventually he will end it by never texting you again. Save yourself time and heartache by not texting a guy first—ever. This *Rule* also applies to instant messages, Facebook, and e-mails, as we will discuss in later chapters.

You might be thinking, "Seriously? Even today a guy still has to reach out to me first?" or "Everything is more casual these days. This generation is different!" We understand how you feel. It may seem crazy or way too strict not to talk to or text guys first, but it really works! When we told women fifteen-plus years ago not to initiate a relationship by speaking to or calling men first, they also reacted with utter shock. But they quickly got over it when they realized the results.

Sometimes successful women are the biggest *Rules*-breakers. They argue that their MBA or graduate degrees give them license to pursue men like they pursue careers and condos. But a *Rules*-y businesswoman knows that work and love are just not the same. You still have to let guys make the first move.

Unfortunately, many smart young women find this *Rule* out the hard way. Abby, a twenty-one-year-old journalism

major, thought *The Rules* were so yesterday. She had read
our first book in her freshman year, but didn't feel it applied
to her because she liked doing her own thing. So when David
walked into the bar and didn't come over to her, she went
over to him. She thought, "What's the worst that can happen?" She liked everything about David's look, from his long,
wavy hair to his Polo shirt with the collar up to his sports
jacket and loafers. He was "exactly her type," she told us.

She said "Hey" and nothing more. David said "Hey" back
and bought her a drink. They talked for two hours and "had
insane chemistry." They liked the same music (Coldplay),
food (sushi), vacation spot (Bermuda), sport (basketball), and
TV shows (*Mad Men* and *Law & Order*). They "even held
hands for a few minutes" before saying good-bye. She felt
chills going up and down her spine. This guy could be The
One! They exchanged numbers and he said he would call her.

The next day he texted her, "Nice meeting you. Just moved
into a great one-bedroom. What do you think of coming over
one night? I'll cook." Abby wrote back two minutes later,
"Sure, when?" David wrote back two minutes later, "Busy
with new job, will get back to you" and then he didn't write
back for a week. When he wrote next, it was late at night from
work. Abby's best non-*Rules* friend suggested she ask him
how his job was going. She told her, "If he's so busy with his
new job, it would be nice of you to ask." So Abby texted him,
"Is your new job really stressful?" and he wrote back, "Yes,
thanks for asking," but never followed through on his invite.

Abby contacted us, confused about why David dropped
the ball. She toyed with the idea of sending him another
friendly text, but decided to e-mail us instead. She didn't
understand why he would suggest getting together and not

follow through, especially when she had been so nurturing. She was sure that she had found her perfect soul mate and couldn't figure out what went wrong.

We carefully went over the whole evening and explained that he may have been her exact look and personality type, but apparently she was not his. If she had been, he would have walked over to *her*, spoken to her first, and followed up with a real date. Because she spoke to him first, she created an interaction that may never have happened, and because *she* kept it going, she was completely baffled as to why he was not more responsive. But we aren't! The reason you shouldn't speak to a guy first is to find out what he will do on his own. If a guy doesn't make the first move, he doesn't make other things happen either, like texts and calls and actual dates. A guy you speak to first will let the ball drop because he never wanted that ball to begin with—he was just being polite or was flattered. Playing by this *Rule*, you get to see if he would have approached you, a short brunette, the tall blonde across the room, or no one at all because he has a girlfriend and just wanted to have a drink. Abby was crushed to hear the truth, but she conceded that we were right and that's why David had disappeared into thin air. And by the way, she never heard from him again.

Perhaps you're thinking, "Of course I would never speak to a guy first like Abby did—or even call a guy because that seems aggressive—but texting is different. Everyone texts these days." We get it and you can totally text a guy back, as you'll see in *Rule #3*, but you cannot text a guy *first*.

Now let's go over the second texting intention we mentioned earlier. What if a guy spoke to you first, called you first, and took you out on a date, but then you didn't hear

Fool Yourself If You Must

Sure, you *think* you won't text a guy, but when you're feeling lonely on a Friday night and there's a Katherine Heigl rom-com playing on TV, we know the temptation can be a little too much to resist. To fight the urge you get every time you scroll past his number in your contacts list, we suggest a simple fix: change his name. It might be hard to stop yourself from sending a flirty message to "Jake" or "Ethan," but it's much easier to bypass "DON'T DO IT!" or "HE'LL THINK YOU'RE CLINGY!" If this tactic still doesn't do the trick—which it might not on those nights when you're feeling especially eager—then delete his number from your phone. The temptation will be gone altogether, and your cool and casual reputation will remain intact. Another option is to find something positive to keep you busy and distract you. Go to the gym, give yourself a mani/pedi, or call up a friend and get out of the house! Sometimes just sitting around gives you too much time to think, too much time to stare at your phone, and too much time to "accidentally" press send. You will never regret *not* texting him, but there's a big chance you will regret it if you do.

—Rules Daughters

from him again? Would it be okay to shoot him a quick text, "Hey, I had a fun time with u. How are u? What happened with your promotion?" No, it would not. Such a message would make it obvious that you are looking to make contact and waiting for him to ask you out again. Be honest with yourself and *don't text him first after a date*!

Like it or not, after a date, you have to wait for a guy to reach out and ask you out again. You cannot remind him that you exist. If you text him without hearing from him first, you will prolong a relationship that may actually be over. If he doesn't call or text you after the date, it's not because he is too busy at work, his dog is sick, he is relocating, or he's visiting his cousin in the hospital—he's just not interested. Hence, no text.

Women might argue, "But how will he know I like him if I don't text him to follow up after a date?" He will know you like him because you went on the date with him and you will return *his* text. To text first is to initiate contact. He may feel flattered for a minute, but then he will feel bored and move on to the next girl he really wanted and texted first.

Women who have a crush become positively ingenious when it comes to finding reasons to text a guy first. They want to thank him for drinks or dinner. They want to invite him to hear their friend's band play at a club. They conveniently have two courtside tickets to his favorite basketball team or to a Broadway show he casually mentioned. They are going to be in his neighborhood or near his office and want to stop by. They are thinking about joining his gym and wanted to get a quick tour. Their friends are throwing them a thirtieth-birthday party and they want to send him an Evite. They want to wish him a safe trip to California. The list goes on and on. The bottom line is you have to restrain yourself from texting a guy first for *any* reason. It is pursuing, it doesn't work, and it is a waste of time.

Mandy, a twenty-six-year-old nurse, e-mailed us asking if she could text a guy who she had been on and off with for a year (a scenario no *Rules* Girl would put up with!) to say their favorite group was playing in Atlantic City. "I won't call him, but can I just shoot him a quick text? Would that be so bad? New Year's Eve is coming up and I really want a date." We went over the whole relationship. They were introduced at a party and talked for three hours that night. He told her he had just ended a relationship and was "not looking for anything serious." They hooked up about eight times after that, all last-minute dinners and booty calls. The last time she heard from him had been two months earlier when he needed to vent about his ex. After he vented, they had sex.

Of course she shouldn't contact him! A text would inevitably lead to a flurry of friendly messages and last-minute dates—and if she wanted a serious relationship, this wasn't it. It would be obvious that the text was just an excuse to contact him because New Year's Eve was two weeks away and she didn't have a date. Furthermore, we explained that if she texted him and he wrote back, she would be getting the false impression that he was interested. Then her fantasy relationship would continue, preventing her from meeting guys who were truly interested in her and asking her out every week. Mandy agreed but then asked if she could at least send him one last text saying the relationship wasn't working for her and to never contact her again.

Still no! Closure is yet another excuse women use to get in touch with a guy and is not *The Rules*. Believe it or not, you actually have to wait until a guy texts you to turn him down or dump him so you can get your closure. Mandy fought a good fight but finally agreed that her motive should be to play hard to get. Obviously, though, you can't play hard to get with a guy who is not trying to get you. After e-mailing us and *not* texting her fantasy guy, Mandy joined a gym and signed up for an online dating site. Ultimately, not texting him was liberating: she gave up a bad habit and made room for better things.

Closure is one of the biggest *fake* reasons women give for making contact with a guy they never had a serious relationship with. They have been on only a few dates and then have not heard from him in weeks or months—he is probably dating someone else—but they need their closure anyway. (In our first book and in *Rule #6*, we explain when a call or text for closure *is* appropriate.) Closure for a guy is never calling or texting or seeing a girl again. A guy doesn't need a final conversation or text chat. In his mind, it's just over—that's good enough for him. But for many women, a relationship is not technically over until they have gotten everything off their chest. One woman we know texted a guy who ended their one-month relationship, saying that she felt used and accusing him of stringing her along, even though he never said they were exclusive or told her he loved her. She felt she couldn't move on without saying those things to him. We would have told her to write it but never hit the send button.

When you finally stop making excuses to text a guy first, you will be on your way to becoming a *Rules* Girl. At first you may feel empty, the way you feel when you start sticking to your diet and skip dessert, but when you don't give in to the temptation, you will feel empowered and free. You may be able to bluff yourself and well-meaning friends with reasons to text a guy, but no *Rules* Girl would buy into it. It's so much better getting a text from a guy than sending one!

Don't Ask Guys Out by Text, Facebook, Instant Messenger, or Any Other Way

THIS *RULE* CAN be difficult because we are essentially telling you to be passive about dating, while you are powerful in so many other areas of your life. You may have a master's degree and an expense account. You may be president of your sorority. You may have your own blog and hundreds of Twitter followers. You may sit on the board of your condo association. You may fly business class to Europe for sales meetings.

But here, we are telling you that you cannot even suggest having coffee with a guy. Remember, the premise of *The Rules* is that men and women are not the same romantically. Men love a challenge and the feeling of pursuing. A woman can be as smart or smarter than a man; she can make the same money as a man or even more money than him; she can get a job doing whatever she wants—but when it comes to dating, she cannot be the aggressor without eventually regretting it. Just like texting or talking to a guy first, asking them out destroys the chase and rarely works out, as men know exactly what their type/look is and go after it. If you ask a guy out, he may say yes to be polite, for sex, or out of boredom, but eventually he will drop you for the girl he really likes.

Most women agree that it would be unfeminine and potentially embarrassing to ask a guy out on a weekend date, but they rationalize asking guys out on other nights of the week and on dates that might not be so obvious. A girl might text a guy and his group of friends, "Hey, why don't you all come to the pre-game at my apartment?" and not think she is asking him out. She may secretly be hosting this pre-game or throwing her BFF a thirtieth-birthday party just so she can invite her crush and think nothing of it. She might e-mail that cute guy from English Lit class and say, "Hey, do you want to go over our essays together?" Or if she knows he likes a particular sports team, she might say, "We're all watching the Giants game at Maggie's later—want to come hang out?" Sure, it's not formal, it's for a specific reason, and it's in a group setting, but none of these details change the fact that you *are* asking him out.

Women come up with all kinds of excuses to see guys they like. They are having a Super Bowl party, even though they've never watched a football game in their life. They are having an Oscar party in their apartment or a fund-raiser for some rare disease. Their power is out and they are frightened. Would he mind coming over? Their computer is down and they can't get their printer set up. Could he take a quick look? These are all subtle ways of getting a guy to be with them; they may not be as blatant as suggesting getting together for drinks or dinner, but they still don't work. Some women spend hours on the phone with their girlfriends concocting the perfect reason to reach out to a guy!

Women asking guys out under the guise of being cool and casual is all too common. Amber, thirty, met Jeremy, thirty-three, at a party. Jeremy spoke to her first, got her number, and texted her to meet for drinks later in the week. He also friended her on Facebook. They met for drinks and then she never heard from him again. Amber really liked him and desperately wanted to figure out a way to contact him again that wasn't too obvious. She knew she couldn't ask him out on a date, but she thought it wouldn't be so bad to message him on Facebook about her BFF's upcoming Christmas party, which they had schemed to throw for the sole purpose of seeing him again. She wrote, "Thanks for drinks. Not sure what you are doing Friday night, but my friend is having a big party. Let me know if you want to join me—no pressure!" Amber spent half an hour crafting the perfect Facebook message with her friend so she did not sound like she was asking him out! Two minutes later Jeremy wrote back, "Cool, would love to come." He showed up and they had a great time—but she still never heard from him again after that.

That's when Amber e-mailed us for help. We explained that the relationship was over when she didn't hear from him after drinks. Facebook messaging him an invitation to the party was asking him out and was against *The Rules*. Just because it was via the internet and not for a Saturday night dinner date does not mean it was okay. If it's not his idea to hang out with you, then you're asking him out. Most importantly, you're forcing the relationship to carry on longer than it should.

Let's be honest here! If you have to figure out ways to make a guy be with you, the relationship won't hold up long term. Amber later found out—through Facebook—that Jeremy and his ex-girlfriend were back together and *that* was why he never asked her out again. There is always a reason, which is why *Rules* Girls don't try to make anything happen!

Quit Playin' Games

If we've learned anything from the romantic-comedy genre, it's that most guys don't like girls who play games. These days, there may be a lot more games to choose from, but the same *Rule* still applies. You might think it's harmless to start a round of Draw Something with that cutie from chemistry. Maybe you're curious just how big his, um, vocabulary is and decide that a few rounds of Words with Friends might be the best test. But as you already know, a girl should never make the first move— even if that move involves a computerized letter tile. Just as with flirting and texting, it's always best to wait for him to show you that he's interested, and you should never initiate a mobile game. In fact, the best advice we can give here is to avoid playing games altogether—that is, phone games. A *Rules* Girl doesn't waste time with Scramble— she's too busy with her life away from her phone and making dates with the guys who are actually asking! If a guy wants to get your attention, he can call you, text you, or ask you out.

—*Rules Daughters*

Short term, sure, a guy will take you up on the party or movie or study session. But he won't be coming for *you*! Guys will see through these contrived invitations eventually and start to think "desperate" or "aggressive." They will want the girl who is invariably too busy to ask them out or barely seems to notice them!

Remember, a guy likes who he likes and an invitation to a game or party won't change that. If you're his type/look and somewhat of a challenge, he will find you and ask you out. Even if he thinks you're pretty, but not the type he goes for, nothing will make a difference in how he feels about you. The sooner you accept this truth, the sooner you will become a *Rules* Girl!

As unfair and unfeminist as it sounds, a woman can do absolutely nothing to start a relationship. We understand it's frustrating for many women, especially movers and shakers. Some argue, "What's the worst that can happen, that he will say no to drinks—so what?" Wrong. The worst that can happen is that he will say *yes* and date you, have sex with you, and lead you to believe that you are in a relationship. But eventually he will dump you for the girl he really likes. So you will have wasted time and possibly gotten your heart broken. We cannot stress this point enough: men were born to do the asking!

So if you have any thoughts of sending that Evite to a guy or quick text to invite him and his friends to drinks after work, think twice—and don't do it! Any energy that is going into manipulating guys to be with you should be used to create your online dating profile and to go to clubs, bars, parties, and singles events where you can meet guys who ask you out. Like it or not, being the one asked out, not the asker, is the only way it works with men!

_____

Don't Sit or Stand next to a Guy First or Flirt with Him First

Wʜɪʟᴇ ᴛᴀʟᴋɪɴɢ ᴛᴏ or texting a guy first is clearly aggressive behavior and not *The Rules*, you might be wondering if sitting next to a guy you like in class or standing next to a guy at a bar or party or flirting with him is okay. Isn't "innocently" sitting or standing or walking over to his area or making flirtatious eye contact relatively benign? No! It shows much more interest than you think!

Such flirtatious behavior is a futile way of trying to get him to notice you—and a complete waste of time. Remember, *The Rules* are about not making anything happen with a guy, because he has to notice you first or you will most likely get hurt. In consultations, many women have said to us that they didn't realize that flirting with a guy first was the crux of their problem. They spent years in therapy talking about the guy and never understood why he sometimes behaved badly and eventually ended the relationship. We help them see it was because they started the relationship. A lightbulb goes on and they can trace the problem back to the first moment they met the guy and flirted with him!

If you ask someone to switch seats with you on a train so you can sit next to a guy you think is cute, you are wasting your time. You will never know if he would have switched seats to sit next to you, and you may be initiating a relationship that was never meant to be. A guy knows within minutes or even seconds of boarding a train or walking into a party who he wants to sit next to or approach, and doesn't need any help figuring it out. So even if you sit next to him or make eye contact from across the aisle, he will still track down the girl he thinks is pretty or is his type.

Women create situations in which they can subtly flirt. They reach for the same item at the grocery store, they wait next to him for a drink at a bar, they purposely brush up against him at a crowded party, or they take the elevator going down instead of up. You can stand next to him all day at the gym, pretending to be waiting for the elliptical machine, and you can put a force field around him, but he will eventually find the girl he likes and walk over to her, chat her up, grab her phone, and even call himself from it so he has her number for sure. Don't even bother! If you see a guy you like, wait for him to walk over to you. That's the only way it works with men!

You are probably wondering how he will know you like him if you don't sit or stand next to him or make eye contact or flash a smile. Many women ask us about flirting techniques and other ways to get a guy to notice them. We don't believe in flirting or staring because it is a dead giveaway of interest—the opposite of being a challenge. A guy knows you are interested if you give him your number when he asks for it and if you say yes when he asks you out. Really, guys don't need you to tap them on the shoulder or even glance in their direction.

You might argue, "But what if he is quiet? Can't I stand next to him if he is a more passive type?" No! We have found that even a shy guy will ask a mutual friend to introduce him to the "cute girl over there." He will point to her and say, "That's the one," and then his friend will bring them together. Or a shy guy will pretend he likes the pretzels that she is standing next to at a party. He will figure out a way to meet her, even if he has to trip her up to get her attention!

Not only should you refrain from doing anything flirty to get his attention, but you should actually do the complete opposite and pretend not to notice him at all. You should look the other way or walk the other way because sometimes it's hard to disguise the fact that you think he is good-looking. It may be written all over your face. And if he notices you staring at him, he will know that you like him. He might typecast you as "easy" and lose interest.

We are not making this up! We have heard countless stories about women who stood next to guys at a bar all night, hoping that would make them take notice. Sometimes such behavior leads to a mercy date or two, but the guy texts only to hook up or he texts to talk about another woman who won't go out with him or who cheated on him. He wants the girl who doesn't give him the time of day! Invariably, standing next to a guy at a bar or party makes you his consolation prize, his free therapist—not his girlfriend. Sometimes flirting first does lead to a longer relationship, but there is usually some fundamental problem. There are fights or miscommunication or intimacy issues.

Lexi, twenty-six, told us she would never approach a guy at a bar, but asked what was so wrong with "standing next to him and swaying to the music" to get his attention? Lexi had seen her Matt Damon look/type and thought her dance moves would catch his eye. She danced around him for fifteen minutes while he gazed around the room. He finally looked her way and asked her if she wanted a drink. She said sure triumphantly. She was proud of herself for not speaking to him first and confident that he was interested. He talked about his ex-girlfriend the whole night and then asked for her number and said he would text her soon. But he didn't, and she wanted to know why not. We explained that he was never interested in the first place—just bored. We told Lexi that swaying next to him created a conversation that would never have happened otherwise, that got her hopes up, and that wasted her time. He spoke to her the way you speak to someone you sit next to on a plane or in a doctor's waiting room: simply out of politeness.

So lest you think you can get into a guy's heart by invading his space, think again. If you have to even walk over to his area, forget it. He is supposed to notice you and find you on his own. The guy who likes you will ask if the seat next to *you* is taken or ask the other guy to move. He will be obvious about it and you won't have to wonder if you're reading him right. He will sit or stand next to you, pretend he drinks coffee so he can wait in line near you at Starbucks, and get your name and number. So think twice before "innocently" sitting or standing next to a guy in class or flirting with a guy at a business networking seminar or museum. *Rules* Girls wait for guys to sit and stand next to *them*. They don't make anything happen or waste time, and neither should you!

Wait at Least Four Hours to Answer a Guy's First Text and a Minimum of 30 Minutes Thereafter

Now you are probably wondering how and when to respond to a guy who *does* text you first. By far the most frequently asked question we get from clients and readers is "I just got a text from a guy I like. When do I write back and what do I say? *Please get back to me ASAP.*"

We all know intellectually that this question is not a real dating emergency. We have true emergency consultations like finding messages from another woman on a guy's phone or a boyfriend walking out after a fight. Obviously, we drop everything to help these clients. Yet there is something about receiving a first text from a cute guy that feels like life and death. A little bell goes off, bringing about a sense of urgency to answer it. We live in an instant-gratification society, and texting is the pièce de résistance.

All *Rules* Girls know not to call men and to rarely return their calls, a *Rule* that still applies today. But technology has changed so much in the last fifteen years that a text cannot always be treated in the exact same way. After discussing with our daughters and through many consultations, we realized some major differences. A guy will call again if he doesn't get you, but texting is sort of like a phone call that reaches you every time: there's never a bad time for either party and it's never intrusive. If you don't text back at all, he may not know you are waiting for another text or even a phone call. He may just interpret it as a rejection—as if you actually said, "No, thanks." Or he may think you are playing some kind of a game.

Indeed, not answering a guy's text at all or taking too long to do so when the whole world is glued to their phones will raise all kinds of red flags: Did she read *The Rules*? Is she not interested? Or is she just pretending not to be interested? We want to avoid any such possible problems.

Before our first book came out, no one questioned a woman when she took hours or even a day or two to call a guy back or even rarely returned his calls. But for the last fifteen years or so, with the popularity of our book and its infiltration into our culture and lexicon—*The Rules* has been mentioned on sitcoms, talk shows, and in magazines and newspapers—guys sometimes get suspicious that you are playing a game if you don't contact them back in a reasonable amount of time. All the more reason, we are saying, not to ignore texts or wait days to text back. Don't be *impossible* to get. Don't give guys reasons to find you rude or difficult before the first date. We have interviewed guys on this subject, and while most said that not hearing back from a woman for hours wouldn't stop them from asking her out, they felt that not hearing back at all would be irksome and a possible sign that she was not interested or employing some dating strategy. As Oprah famously said on her show, "Guys like a *Rules* Girl, they just don't want it to be because she read a book." We don't want to teach women to insult men!

Our official answer about when to respond to a first text is to wait somewhere between four and twenty-four hours, depending on your age. Four hours is for the younger set—for those in college and women in their early to mid-twenties who grew up with texting and Facebook. The older you are, the longer you should try to wait. For example, a thirty-year-old should wait more like twelve hours, and a forty-plus-year-old should wait a day to reply. (See Text-Back Times chart on pp. 66–67.)

But it's a little more complicated than that. If a guy texts you for the first time at, say, 9 or 10 a.m., you wouldn't write back exactly four hours later while you're at school or work because, theoretically, you are not checking your phone all day long. You would wait until after you clock out and leave, whenever that is. If our suggested minimum wait time falls during the middle of your day, keep waiting! Remember that it is a *minimum* and you can't be expected to look at your phone all the time—or give the impression that you do.

If a guy texts you for the first time in the late afternoon, say at 3 or 4 p.m., you should write back later in the evening, after the time you would be at happy hour or dinner with friends. You can even wait until the next morning—what if you got home late from a movie? In this case, you're giving the impression that you're out doing something fun in the evenings rather than sitting around and fiddling with your phone.

If a guy first texts you after 8 p.m., you should not write back four hours later at midnight, even if you are in the younger age group. You're better off waiting until the next day to avoid late-night texting. In this case, you should write back on your way to class or work the next morning.

These text-back times do not apply to weekends, specifically from Friday at 6 p.m. to Sunday at 6 p.m.; this zone is a "blackout period." Just like airlines have blackout periods in which you can't use your frequent-flier points, so do *Rules* Girls! Weekends are a dead zone. You're unavailable, you're unreachable, you're busy, you're gone! But don't get mad that he's texting you on Saturday. He may have been spoiled by non-*Rules* Girls who put up with or even initiate weekend text chatfests—but you aren't one of them! Don't text lecture him with "Why are you texting me on Saturday? Why didn't you just ask me out by Wednesday for Saturday?" Instead, silently show him that you are not available by not responding at all during the weekend so he knows he must make plans in advance in the future. You can text him back on Sunday night, "Thanks, sounded good, but I already had plans." The *only* exception to this *Rule* is if he already asked you out by Wednesday for Saturday night and is texting during the dead zone to confirm plans. Otherwise, you are blocked out from casual texting on the weekends.

There is, however, one exception to waiting: if he needs an answer right away because he wants to buy concert tickets or something else time-sensitive and needs to make sure the date is good for you, you can quickly write back, "Hey, the 14th at 8 p.m. sounds great tx!" But *do not* abuse this exception or use it as an opportunity to start an unnecessary longer conversation.

Most women, especially those who don't know that dating is strategic, text back men in nanoseconds. So we had to come up with a sensible text-back-time plan that women of all ages can use to delay their natural tendency to respond too quickly and to write more than he does. To a "Hi it's Steven from the other night, how are you?" first text, the average woman will write back in two seconds: "Nice to hear from you! Actually I'm on my lunch break now so heading over to the library to check out a self-help book my friend told me about lol. My car needed to be inspected so I left it at the shop this am. So I'm just walking everywhere today. What's up with you?" These women are spoiling guys now more than ever. Remember, it's just a first text from a new guy! All he wrote was "How are you?" He did not ask for your life story. If you took four hours and wrote back a brief response, it would be absolutely fine. No big deal. In other words, don't interrupt your physics lab, yoga class, or business meeting to answer his text. It can wait! *He* can wait. You feel compelled to text back paragraphs right away...lest what? Another girl will text him and take him away with her quick and witty response? More likely, he will think you are busy and/or with other guys—and that would be a good thing.

It's important to realize that for a guy, not every text is as earth-shattering as it is for you. He could be texting you while filling his tank at the gas station. For guys, texting can be fun, like a sport or video game. But for a girl, a text from a cute guy is really special, like winning the lottery. In the midst of twenty other messages from girlfriends, coworkers, her parents, and her sister, there's a text from the guy she really likes and it's all she can think about.

Before reading our book, she writes back immediately. Within an hour of hasty texting back and forth, they know more about each other than would have been divulged on a first date. During a lull, she goes over the conversation to dissect its meaning—she might forward it to her friends to understand exactly what he is saying. She studies it like an exam paper or the Scriptures. Typically this woman ends up in a chatfest that doesn't lead to a date—certainly not a Saturday night date—and then contacts us for help. She doesn't understand why her relationships are casual or fizzle out, despite a promising he-spoke-to-her-first beginning. She thought she should be available and text guys back nonstop to keep them interested. Not true! *That's* why we are writing this book. Stop treating texts like an emergency that requires an immediate response. After you read this chapter, texting back in nanoseconds should feel like touching a hot stove!

There's another critical piece to this *Rule*: after you do text back, limit the conversation to fifteen minutes or ten total exchanges. This strategy makes him wonder what you are doing, creates anticipation, and forces him to ask you out to have a relationship. All these things are good, so don't feel guilty about them!

Brittany, twenty-two, met a guy at a party who walked over to her—a promising beginning! He got her number and texted her the next day, "Hey there, so glad we met last night. I was wondering how your day is going." What was her next move? Four hours later she wrote back: "Nice meeting you too! Work is good but crazy busy!" She had wanted to ask him how his day was going but we advised her against it, reminding her that she wanted him to ask her out. We told her to be witty but brief to prevent endless chatter. He wrote back five minutes later, "What do you do for work?" She wrote back thirty minutes later, "I'm a pharmaceutical sales rep." He wrote back three minutes later, "Do you get to try out all the drugs for free? haha." She wrote back twenty minutes later, "nope, lol." Two minutes later he wrote, "So what do you like to do for fun? Maybe we can go to the movies. Are you free this Saturday night?" She wrote back thirty minutes later, "Yes, that would be great." Mission accomplished! No chatfest and this *Rules* Girl got a date!

Stacey, twenty-four, had to work a little harder to rope in a guy. She got this text at 8 p.m. on a Tuesday night from a guy she had met at a bar: "Great meeting you last night. That place has really delicious appetizers. How are you doing?

Any fun plans this weekend?" First she dissected it on her own. She wasn't 100 percent sure if he was asking her out or just chatting. With his chitchatty questions, she was worried about it turning into a textfest with no date. She *wanted* to write back, "No, this weekend is really wide open. Why, what are you doing?" Absolutely not! First of all, he did not ask her out directly or suggest a specific night, so it would be presumptuous to assume that. Because he sent his message after 7 p.m., she waited until the next morning and wrote, "Nice meeting you too...nothing definite for the weekend yet!"

He wrote back two minutes later: I thought maybe we could get together.

Stacey waited 30 minutes and wrote back: Sure, that sounds great!

He wrote back: What were you thinking? When is good for you?

Stacey waited 20 minutes and wrote back: When did you have in mind?

He wrote back five minutes later: Saturday night for dinner?

Stacey waited 30 minutes this time and wrote back: OK, great!

The highlights here: Never assume a guy is asking you out, and don't volunteer your schedule. Make him pin you down for a specific night. And of course, don't text him back immediately, and when you do respond, mix it up and write fewer words than he does. In addition, never double text (write twice before he responds once), as you will come across as too eager.

Text- Back Times

Not sure how soon or long to wait to answer a guy's subsequent texts? Look no further! Here is our chart for minimum response times by age with detailed explanations.

Age	Minimum Text-Back Time	Why
18–22 years old	30 minutes Want to really catch his attention? Wait an hour!	If you are 18 to 22 years old and in a committed, exclusive relationship, you should text back after 30 minutes, but can text more regularly than with a guy you just met, but you still have to be somewhat mysterious and end it first.
23–25 years old	One hour Want to really catch his attention? Wait two hours!	Women 23 to 25 years old are usually busy working and living in their own apartments. They have real things going on like business meetings and a commute and rent and bills to deal with, so it would be completely realistic to take an hour to get back to a guy, and it wouldn't be so bad to make a guy wait two hours! *Rules* Girls do not check their texts in the middle of a meeting with a client or while driving home from work. The first is not smart and the second is dangerous.

Age	Minimum Text-Back Time	Why
26–30 years old	Two hours Want to really catch his attention? Wait three hours!	Women 26 to 30 years old are not only working and being social, but they have even more responsibilities than recent college graduates. Perhaps they have a secretary or supervise an assistant and have to do important things like check their balances online or meet their quotas. They are also hopefully going to parties and clubs and on dates, so they can't text back all day long either.
31 and over	Three hours Want to really catch his attention? Wait four hours!	Most women 31 years old and older want to get married. They have important jobs and other responsibilities and interests such as mortgages, volunteer work, and nieces and nephews, and have no time to text back men who just want to text and not ask them out for Saturday night dates.

All texts, especially the first one from a new guy, should be responded to with fewer words than he wrote. For example, if he writes, "Hey what's up? Wanna go out sometime?" you should write back, "Sure, that sounds like fun." Do not write back, "Sure, that would be great. Work is kind of crazy, but I am free this Thursday night and all weekend and I know a really cool happy hour place." That would be too many words as well as too eager. For whatever reason, women can blow men out of the water with their verbiage. By writing more than a guy, you become the more interested party, and thus the pursuer, because the more words you use, the more interested and available you seem. Less is more! Remember, in the beginning you want to seem too busy to text immediately or to text a lot so *he* has to chase *you*.

When we help women with answering subsequent texts, we ask how she and the guy met, their ages, whether they are in fact dating or just texting a lot, how long they have been seeing each other, and what the current situation is. No matter the circumstances, a *Rules* Girl should not text back in less than thirty minutes or three hours, depending on her age. These are minimums! Even if a guy is texting to confirm a date, you can wait an hour to write back. Remember, you don't live to text—you have a life!

Remember, these text-back times are not for answering a guy's first text. That should *always* be a minimum of four hours or more. But once a text conversation gets going, you should *not* rigidly stick to the response time for your age group. Not only would that be taking too long, but it would also be too predictable. You have to mix it up so he doesn't know what you are doing and doesn't suspect you are employing any kind of dating strategy. If you are twenty years old, after your first response, you would then text back in thirty minutes, then five minutes to answer the next text, and then maybe ten to twenty minutes for the next. Then, when he is expecting another text in twenty minutes, throw in an hour-long wait so that you stay unpredictable. Keep him checking his phone in anticipation! While a guy might be caught off guard the first or second time you don't text back right away, if you don't text back right away, he will come to expect that and know you are busy doing other things and like to take your time. He will make up excuses as to why you didn't write back faster. He will say, "You are so bad with your phone!"

When a guy doesn't text or text back, women make up excuses for him: "He must be really busy with work," or "He's probably watching a football game," or "His phone must have died." But if *she* doesn't text back right away herself, she feels she is being rude or cold or playing games. Don't you have a life? Aren't you busy, too? How can a guy prove whether you are doing *The Rules* or just busy? He can't.

If you have BlackBerry Messenger, iMessage, or a similar program, a guy might be able to tell if you have read his text. If you don't respond within a few minutes, he could be insulted that you read his text and didn't write back quickly. If you have this feature on your phone, don't read his text until you are ready to answer it.

Sara, a twenty-seven-year-old speech therapist in Seattle, met a hunky realtor at a bar. He spoke to her first, asked for her number, and texted her the next day and the next day and the day after that, but never asked her out. She thought she was doing *The Rules*, but couldn't figure out where she was going wrong, so she sent us the conversations.

Texting versus Calling: A Great Debate?

Obviously nothing is as disrespectful as a text-message breakup (and hopefully you'll never experience one firsthand), but do the same *Rules* apply to a text-message ask-out? The idea of a guy asking a girl out via text message may sound a little juvenile—like those middle-school notes you'd find in your locker that read, "Do you like me?" with boxes for yes and no—but we don't think so. These days, it doesn't matter whether a guy calls, texts, or even e-mails to ask you out, as long as he asks you right. Especially if you've been texting each other already (which, let's be honest, we're sure you have been), he shouldn't have to give you a call when he wants to pop this particular question. To be honest, wouldn't it be a little awkward if he did? Who even talks on the phone anymore?! The point is, he asked you out—congratulations!

—*Rules Daughters*

Him: Hey great meeting you last night. How do you like Seattle? Very different from Florida, huh?

Her: I like it a lot—there's a Starbucks on every corner!

Him: I don't go to bars a lot, just wanted to chill with some friends, but then I got lucky and met you.

Her: Thanks. I'm not a big bar goer either.

Him: You're very pretty. I wouldn't think you would have problems meeting guys.

Her: Thanks, you're sweet. So sorry, but I have to take a call for work.

Him: OK, we should get together sometime…

Her: That sounds great!

Next Day

Him: Hey, you mentioned you like sushi. Maybe we can go for sushi sometime.

Her: Sure!

Him: Good to know, I've been looking for a sushi buddy. You also mentioned last night you have a sister in LA. I love LA. Have you been there recently?

Her: Yes, I went to LA and Arizona last month.

Him: Cool. What did you do there?

Her: We hung out at the beach. Next client just got here… Gotta run!

Him: OK TTYL

The Day after That

Him: So what do you like to do when you're not working?

Her: Rent movies, work out, meet friends…

Him: Did you see the latest Mission Impossible? It was great.

Her: Yes! I really like Tom Cruise, he's so funny.

Him: I'm burnt out here. I'm talking to some headhunters.

Her: Good luck! My boss just walked in…

Him: OK let's make plans.

Her: Sounds good!

Although the hunky realtor spoke to Sara first, got her number, and texted her first, and her *Rules*-y responses were properly timed and shorter than his, this was a case of text chatting gone wild. We told her that at this point, the only way he would ask her out was if she ignored his texts completely. She was shocked. "I thought I was allowed to text a little. Isn't ignoring him rude?" No, it's not rude—you're just busy and have a life. If a guy wants to ask all these questions about LA and movies, he can ask over sushi!

Sara agreed to try it. The next morning when cute realtor texted, "Hey, how's your day going?" she didn't write back. When he texted later that afternoon, "Meeting with headhunter. Wish me luck!" she ignored it. That night he texted "What r u up to?" she ignored it again. The next morning he finally texted, "Hey there stranger, maybe we can meet for sushi this weekend." She waited two hours and wrote back, "Sure, that sounds good!" Two minutes later he asked, "How is Friday night after work?" And thirty minutes after that she wrote, "Perfect." And that was it. They finally had a first date and many dates after that.

If a guy is texting but not asking you out, you have to cut him off until he gets that you are too busy to just chat endlessly. This freezing-him-out plan is not about playing games but about boundaries, self-esteem, and self-worth. Men will eat up your time if you let them! Many women waste hours or days politely texting guys back throughout the day, yet find themselves dateless on Saturday night. *Rules* Girls don't put up with aimless chitchat. Remember, the point of texting a guy back is to get a date or to be in a relationship—not to talk all day. But what if a guy stops texting you and never asks you out because you didn't answer every text? Did you do anything wrong? No, he just wasn't that crazy about you to begin with—he's a time waster. Next!

We know that waiting won't always be easy. In fact, it might even get harder when you are in a relationship and he knows your schedule or sees that you answer your girlfriends' texts in two minutes! When you are with him, we suggest leaving your phone in your bag and not holding it in your hand all night, so he doesn't think you are glued to it.

Don't show any interest in your phone or become animated or giddy and say, "Oh my G-d my BFF just posted the funniest photo" when you get a text. If you want to make it seem plausible that you are slow to reply, then don't seem obsessed with your phone.

We are not telling you to be disingenuous, but if you want a guy to stare at his phone wondering when you are going to text him back, if you want a guy to dream about you and think about what you are doing when you are not with him, and if you want a guy's heart to pound while waiting for you to text him back, then don't answer him so fast. Making him wait to hear from you will make him think about you *more*, not less. And isn't that what you want?

TTYL: Always End Everything First—Get Out of There!

IN OUR FIRST book, we told you to end phone calls first. The same *Rule* applies to every new form of communication that has cropped up since then, and to dates, too. We call it "getting out of there." Why? So you don't talk too much, and leave him wanting more! Remember that sometimes reverse psychology works best. If you want more from a guy, give him less. The busier you seem to be, the more curious or interested he'll become.

While all of this newfangled—or old—communication, from calls on the landline to video chatting on the computer to text chats to Skype, is about wowing a guy with your fascinating personality and showing him how cultured and witty you are, it's also about "getting out of there" in ten to fifteen minutes of active chatting so that he is forced to ask you out if he wants to continue the relationship. Instant messaging and FaceTime are not dates!

Some women feel rude or disingenuous about ending chats first, but it's not a game. Doing so indicates that you have a full schedule and healthy boundaries. Are you with a friend, at a meeting, at the gym, in class, or with your book club? Guys who wonder where you're off to are more likely to text again and ask you out, even if they claim that they are receptive to girls who chat openly and frequently.

If you are worried about being perceived as abrupt, remember that guys have no problem ending a conversation first. You could be in the middle of a great chat and then BAM, he says he has to go, the football game just started or his roommate walked in. Remember that guys can be your adversary. They have the power to turn it off in an instant, to never text again, or to never ask you out. You can protect yourself by ending every interaction first.

Let's be honest here. It's not that you can't end a conversation first—it's that you won't. You become so obsessed in a conversation that it's as if you are in a trance. Maybe your BFF is sitting right next to you screaming, "Stop texting already!" and actually tries grabbing your phone out of your hand, but to no avail. Or maybe you grab your phone back and continue texting. You ignore your girlfriends or family while sneaking texts under the table at restaurants or by excusing yourself to go to the bathroom. Your friends and parents eventually get fed up.

Girls have convinced themselves that they will lose a guy if they end the chat too quickly. They are afraid he will lose interest and move on to the next girl if they "get out of there" first. Of course, we know the opposite is true. If a guy likes your look, spoke to you first, called or texted you first, and you end the chats early after ten to fifteen minutes of active back-and-forth, he will try you again or ask you out. If he *really* stops texting you, it's not because you "got out of there"—it's because he just doesn't like you enough. You don't want to keep chatting with someone who isn't interested enough to text you again!

You can say, "I only have one bar left on my phone" or "Gotta take this call" or "Have to study" or "Work is crazy" or "Spin class starts in five minutes." You don't have to have the perfect conversation ender—anything will do! There's no reason to feel bad. Remember that even therapists go by the clock and tell patients in the middle of a good cry, "Your time is up." Why can't you end a casual text conversation first? If you can't figure out something creative, just write, "Sorry, gotta go!" and turn off your phone for a few minutes to create space and distance—just like we told you in our first book to set an egg timer to end calls. If you truly feel incapable of ending a conversation on your own, ask a friend to send you a reminder. If you know you can't trust yourself, don't answer him at all. Leave your phone in your bag, in the car, or in another room.

And don't wait for that perfect moment or lull in the conversation to end the texting. Who knows when that will be? Just keep track of time and end the chat first—"G2GO!" Don't run the risk of his shutting it down first. You will be the one wondering why he had to go and you will start spinning it into something bad in your head! If he ends the conversation first, you might feel so insecure about the relationship that you text him again later to make sure everything is okay, and wind up breaking another *Rule*! It's like fairy dust: when you don't let him end interactions first, you somehow cast a spell on him and he always wants you more.

Tips for keeping the conversation short: Always write less than he does. Don't ask too many questions. Try to answer his questions in a sentence or two but in a witty way. Don't introduce too many new topics, lest a textfest develop. In an attempt to bond with a guy or to catch his interest, a woman will keep a conversation going by answering his questions in great detail, asking him questions, and introducing many new topics. Here is an example of what *not* to do:

Him: Hey, what's up?

Her: Just studying, I have a biology test tomorrow. My roommate is sick. She got so wasted over the weekend. She threw up all over the new rug in the bathroom. I told her not to have more than one drink, but she never listens!

Him: Bummer. Who's your teacher for bio?

Her: Rinaldi. He's the worst. My friend Jackie is in the class and hates him too. Do you know Jackie?

Him: He's such a pain in the ass. I had him last year.

Her: I know. I should have switched. I made such a mistake. Maybe you can help me study?

Him: So I guess you're going to be up late?

Her: Yeah, this is looking like an all-nighter. What's up with you?

Him: Exams, but it's cool. I'm more worried about the football game on Saturday.

Her: I'll be there. When does it start?

Him: 3 pm on Sunday. Gotta run to the gym!

Her: OK, bye! I'll see you then. What time does it start?

She didn't end it first, she said way too much, and he didn't even make plans to see her. What a waste of time! Here is a much better example of how a texting conversation might play out:

Him: Hey what's up?

Her (30 minutes later): Studying.

Him: Yeah me too. Biology is kicking my ass. So what's up for the weekend? Wanna do something together?

Her (10 minutes later): Sure, that sounds like fun! OK, gotta get back to the books...

This *Rule* applies not only to calls, texts, and all other forms of instantaneous communication, but to dates, too. A first date for a *Rules* Girl is one to two hours for coffee or drinks, or a couple of hours for a study date at the library, not hiking and biking for hours on end or an all-day outing at the beach. Too much too soon is never good for a relationship. Besides, it's easier to end a coffee or drink date in one or two hours than it is to end a day at the beach. That's why we politely decline first dates consisting of dinner *and* a movie or an outing to the amusement park.

A guy will usually come on strong in the beginning and try to get a marathon first or second date if he thinks you'll let him. Even though he initially suggested such a long date, he may think you are too easy and eager, and get bored by the third date—if there even is one. You need to pace the relationship and let him gradually get to know you so he doesn't get too much too soon and move on to the next girl.

Your answer to a guy who suggests driving to the park for a picnic or drinks, dinner, and dancing for a first date would be "Drinks sound good to me!" After one or two hours, you can look at your watch and say, "I'm having a great time, but I really have to get going." If he asks why, you can just say you have a really big day tomorrow. You don't have to say with what—it's none of his business. If you feel that you *must* justify it some way, you can say you are busy with work or have an early-morning session with your trainer. Be as mysterious as you can! If you are in college and your date consists of hanging out at a party or two, end it before he does. Never extend a date with "Let's see what's going on at Club G..."

or "Let's go to another bar..." And even if it's his idea to extend it, you should still say you can't. If you don't follow these *Rules* about getting out of there first, you will not be a challenge. If he wants to spend more time with you, he can and will ask to see you again.

A second date should be three or four hours for dinner. A third date can be dinner and a movie for about five hours. A fourth date can be dinner and a show and coffee afterward for about six hours. But you end *all* these first—you get out of there!

Of course this rule is probably the exact opposite of what you want to do. When you meet a guy you like, you don't want the conversation or date to end! You want to know everything about him right away—his college major or where he works, what car he drives, his favorite sports team, what he likes to do for fun, why his last relationship didn't work out, his five-year plan, and above all, how he feels about you—and you want to tell him your life story, too. But marathon dates kill *any* mystery. Make him want to ask you out—and ask you out again—to learn more!

Don't Answer Texts or Anything Else after Midnight

PART OF *THE RULES* is about silently teaching guys to respect you—and that means setting boundaries, especially when it comes to being reachable. You should not answer calls or messages after midnight, because you are busy or need your beauty sleep or, quite frankly, it's none of his business why! If a guy wants to know what you are doing, he needs to date you. We have found that clients who respond to anything after midnight are asking for trouble: guys inevitably call at all hours, even 1 or 2 a.m., sometimes drunk. But you're a *Rules* Girl. You have a life and are not available 24/7!

Look, we don't live under a rock. We know that guys, especially in college and in their early twenties, like to burn the midnight oil and that late-night calls and texts are the rule, not the exception. But you must put your foot down and ignore him after midnight or you may get caught up in a bad chatfest.

The truth is that nothing good ever happens after midnight. Guys are just looking to set up a hookup—much like they do in person. In our first book, we said that when you go to a bar, club, or party that starts at 9 p.m. you should arrive at 10 p.m. and leave around midnight. Women who hang out until 2 or 4 a.m. to close the place down usually meet drunks, stragglers, and guys looking for one-night stands. Ditto for texts, calls, instant messages, and e-mails after midnight.

When the Clock Strikes Twelve...

Sure, we're up late, but we're up because we're out having fun, hanging on the couch with our girlfriends, or finishing essays for our English class. One of our guy friends confessed that he and his friends made a game of texting five different girls at once after midnight just to see who got a response fastest—and then they challenged each other to see who could sleep with someone first. They literally report to each other afterward and the winner gets a six-pack from each of the two losers! Ew... we were appalled. So, after midnight, IGNORE! Even if he is your crush and you're totally willing to settle for a late-night text, remember—we warned you! Besides, if he's the kind of creep who would do this type of thing, you definitely don't want to be with him anyway.

—*Rules Daughters*

We know this *Rule* is not easy to follow because, thanks to smartphones, dating is more casual these days. But if a guy is calling you after midnight, it's not a date—it's a booty call. He's probably already texted all the other girls he really likes in his contact list and you're his backup choice. He may have sent the exact same text to ten other girls that hour! If that's the case, you're not interested. A *Rules* Girl likes herself too much to be a booty call or a guy's last resort.

We know you are always on your phone, online, or otherwise available—but you don't want to let a guy who texts you after midnight *know* that you're available, so just don't answer. If you write back once, he will think he can *always* message you at crazy hours. If you continue to write back, he might think that you're bored or boring—he might think you're nothing special instead of someone whose nights are filled with fun and friends and maybe even other lucky guys. If you pick up or answer his texts, you might end up in a chatfest and he might convince you to meet up with him at a party or hook up! You don't want to do that, so don't even let yourself be tempted. If you *don't* answer it, the worst thing he can think is that you fell asleep.

Even if you read the text on BlackBerry Messenger or iMessage and he knows that, so what? You don't have to answer every message, especially if it's a late-night one. You might be studying for a test or preparing for a big work meeting. Don't answer your phone! And just know that a guy would have no problem not answering a late-night message—or any message, for that matter.

Being a *Rules* Girl is sort of like being Cinderella. So the next time you are tempted to respond after midnight, think about your gown turning into rags and your golden carriage turning into a pumpkin—that is, your relationship going nowhere.

Rarely Write on His Wall and Other *Rules* for Social Networking Sites

MANY WOMEN ARE understandably unsure how to be social yet still mysterious on networking sites that have made it increasingly harder or almost impossible to play hard to get. After all, Facebook is all about being an open book—between status updates, check-ins, and tagged photos, it seems like the whole world knows what you are up to at all times! But *The Rules* are all about being a challenge and an enigma, and disappearing in between dates so a guy doesn't know what you are doing every minute he is not with you. The premise of Facebook is to connect people, and the premise of *The Rules* is to be elusive. Facebook is like a big, adult playground with no boundaries, while *The Rules* are all about exercising self-control. So how can you be on Facebook and be a *Rules* Girl at the same time?

The tips in this chapter address this very difficult quandary. *The Rules* for Facebook and other social networks are essentially the same as *The Rules* for bars, parties, and other real-life situations: You still want to be mysterious and let him pursue you! Less is always more in your profile, photos, wall posts, likes, comments, and chats. Realize, though, that there will *always* be a way to break *Rules*, be it friending a guy on Facebook, liking his photos, starting a late-night chat, or friending his friends. But when you understand that such actions are really ways of making the first move and creating a non-*Rules* relationship, you will see the wisdom of holding back. We've broken it down into a few easy *Rules* for you to follow.

- **Never friend a guy you really like first.** Friending a guy you really like on Facebook is just like talking to him first. He will know you're interested in him and any challenge will be gone. Friending a guy is the opposite of *The Rules*: it is being the aggressor, it is making the first move, it is trying to get into his world. The only exception is friending guys you are truly only friends with... We mean guys you are not interested in *at all*!

- **Wait twenty-four to forty-eight hours to confirm a friend request from a guy you like.** Do not confirm in nanoseconds when you receive the notification on your iPhone as you would a girlfriend's. Let him think you are busy and running around (which you should be, but more on that later). Some might think you should *never* accept a friend request from a guy you are dating to prevent him from knowing too much about you. We think such action is extreme and actually a misinterpretation of *The Rules*. You are not trying to be *impossible* to get to know—just difficult! Ignoring a friend request is like saying no to a first date: it tells him there is no hope at all, rather than showing you are open to being pursued. Besides, this move can be difficult to pull off, especially if you are young! If you have grown up on Facebook, everything and everyone you know has a Facebook page, and a guy may not understand why you are not accepting his friend request. Remember, we don't want to teach you how to ignore technology, but rather how to date successfully and be mysterious *with* technology. You can always restrict certain items from his view in your privacy settings.

- **Rarely write on a guy's wall—and that includes liking and tagging.** Writing on a guy's wall is like broadcasting to the world that you like him. You might as well be saying, "He's mine, he's mine!" It's too obvious, as if you want everyone in his life, especially other women, to know that he's seeing *you* and that he's taken. Why not just take out a big billboard ad and put your name in a heart with his? Don't create publicity and drama. Additionally, he will know you were thinking about him and poking around his profile.

  Is it *ever* okay to write on a guy's wall? Sure! You can wish him a happy birthday or congratulate him on passing the bar exam or getting a promotion. But you should just write, "Happy Birthday! Have a great day!" or "Congrats!" Nothing way over-the-top like "Happy Birthday to the hottest, most awesome guy in the world. I love you so much!!!!!!!" Keep it short and don't use more than two or three exclamation points. You do not want to come across like an overly enthusiastic cheerleader. Nothing's changed just because you're communicating on the internet. It's always about rarely responding and almost never initiating contact!

  When you are on a date or on the phone, do not bring up his Facebook page like you have been studying it (even if you have) and say things like "I remember you said you liked *Entourage*. Did you see the first season?"

or say anything that is Facebook-inspired, like "I saw your new photos on Facebook. That's so funny what your friend wrote" or "Your Halloween costume was hilarious." It is like Facebook stalking to talk about his page!

Keep in mind that anything you do on Facebook regarding him, whether it's liking or commenting or tagging him in a photo, is making the first move. Don't try to wiggle your way into his world. But if you are in a relationship, you can once in a while reply to a post of his on his wall or post a video that you both laughed at on a date. But we mean *rarely*!

- **Don't always post back if he writes on your wall.** But if you do, wait at least thirty minutes to several hours, depending on your age, as we explain in our Text-Back Times chart on page 66. The truth is, texting, Facebook messages, and posts are all the same. Remember, always do the least and/or write less. If he writes a joke, you can comment back, "haha." If a guy comments on your photo, "gorgeous pic," you don't have to write anything, but if you really want to, just "like" the comment. If a guy complains that you don't respond a lot, you can just tell him you don't go on Facebook that much or say you saw it quickly on your phone and forgot to write back.

- **Share as little as possible.** Guys should have no idea what you are doing in between dates and who you are doing it with. Constant status updates take away all the mystery that is necessary to keep a relationship exciting! With everyone writing to everyone else every five seconds these days, life has become an open book. If you want to be a *Rules* Girl, don't post your status all day long—once or twice a week is plenty—and almost never on the weekends (Friday 6 p.m. to Sunday 6 p.m.). The weekend is a dead zone.

One of the biggest mistakes women who are dating make is constantly posting ordinary/dull status updates. They're "watching X Factor and loving the contestants" or "prepping for a big meeting with the boss" or "meeting college roommate at Friday's," and so on. There is nothing exciting or mysterious about a to-do list. No need to tell the world—including potential dates and boyfriends—about your daily routine. Without so many updates, he can imagine that you are doing interesting things in between your dates, like going to parties or seeing other guys. Why ruin that with hourly status reports? Remember, your life is busy and fabulous—you don't have time to post all these updates anyway!

Additionally, avoid writing life quotes or anything too introspective or negative, like "What goes around, comes around" or "Karma is a bitch." It will sound like you've been hurt or have been reading too many self-help books. Don't write, "So bored" or "Could this day be any longer?" because it will show that you have nothing going on at all! Don't say you are sick or make a frown face or share stories about a car accident or unemployment line. You can make references to events like a social or work party, but don't say where or when or whether you are actually going. You can make inside jokes with friends, but limit posts to three sentences.

Also, write as little information as possible in your profile under such categories as education, work, likes, and interests. You are too busy to write paragraphs about yourself. That is information you can share on dates!

Unfortunately, too many women who are dating use social networking sites like group therapy. A guy looking at your wall will be turned off by TMI quickly and will not find you fascinating or mysterious. He just met you and now he already knows that you hate your job and your other private thoughts and feelings. A guy will run! Baring your soul and displaying your daily ups and downs in a public forum is risky, even downright dangerous. Besides, would you invite people to read your diary?

- **Don't post unflattering photos**—you with cotton candy stuck to your face or with your hair in a towel and mud masque. Don't post these photos, and untag any photos others have posted of you in sweatpants eating pizza in a friend's basement. While they may bring back funny memories or make you laugh, think of how they appear out of context to a new guy. Do they make you look weird or boring? Remember, you want to appear your most attractive on Facebook. It goes without saying that if you don't think you look great in a picture, you will untag it. Surely you don't want *anyone* to see that—cute guy or otherwise! Also, don't post any drinking photos (you holding a plastic red cup at a frat party) and untag any photos of you drinking or looking drunk. Not cool!

If someone else posts a picture, don't be the person to tag the guy you are dating. Let him tag you so that *he* is the one publicizing your relationship. Tagging a guy you're dating is just a sneaky way of telling others you are with him. It's similar to grabbing his hand at a party or putting your arm around his shoulder—it looks like you are trying too hard and might make him uncomfortable.

And one more thing: don't overdo it with photo captions. It shows that you have too much time on your hands if you give every photo a story. You're busy living these things, not flaunting them on Facebook!

- **Don't initiate a Facebook chat.** It's okay to accept a chat, but wait at least four hours to respond if it's a first chat with a new guy. Because Facebook saves the chat, you can simply answer it as a message the next day. If he has initiated a chat before, then wait at least thirty minutes to three hours depending on your age (see that chart again on page 66). A guy should not be able to get you instantaneously. No guy appreciates anything that comes too easily or too quickly; they reach you in every medium in seconds and then lose interest.

  As with texting, after ten or fifteen minutes of active chatting you should end it. If he says, "Hey, what's up?" you can say "Hey" back. Let him initiate the topics, write less than he does, and get out of there first. If a guy asks you out on Facebook, it's okay to say yes, as long as it's by Wednesday for Saturday night or three days in advance for a weeknight date.

- **Be cautious regarding your relationship status.** If you are not dating anyone, don't list your relationship status as single—it's no one's business. Why advertise it? Delete the relationship listing option. It is better to leave your status out altogether because you don't want to show that much interest in the whole subject of relationships. Also, if your status changes from "in a relationship" to "single," your hundreds of friends will be notified and you might be embarrassed.

If you are dating someone, don't post "in a relationship" before he does or make your main photo one of the two of you before he does. We don't think you should post "in a relationship" at all, unless he brings it up or insists that you do. If you initiate either of these things, it might look like you care too much. It could also bring out all the mean girls who want to sabotage your relationship. His ex-girlfriend(s) might see that he is happy with you and try to ruin it by writing on his wall or tagging him in photos. All these things can be avoided by retaining an air of mystery no matter what. But if it's too much for you, then deactivate your profile. Facebook doesn't define you.

- **Don't friend his friends and family first.** Facebook and other social networking sites have made access to everyone he knows all too easy. Don't use these sites as an excuse to waltz into his world. (We will elaborate on this in "Don't Introduce a Guy to Anyone First," in *Rule #17*.) It's aggressive and might scare a guy away! It might freak *them* out too and give them too much information about you! It's like inviting yourself to the family picnic or his sister's wedding. His friends and family should be friending you!

- **De-friend and/or block an ex if he ended the relationship, depending on how badly it ended.** If seeing your ex-boyfriend online or having any contact with him at all is too painful for you, then block him to protect yourself. Some guys want to stay friends on Facebook, but we are not fans of keeping a connection with a guy who broke your heart, because it's too painful, gives you false hope, and wastes your time when you should be moving on. Blocking him will prevent you from seeing his activities on your news feed if you still have mutual friends on Facebook, and will prevent you from seeing his photos (possibly with another woman) and any other information that he leaves open to the public that might upset you. If the relationship ended badly, he might put things on his page to upset you or make his default photo one with a girl there was drama about, which will also be hurtful. To avoid seeing all that, just block him. You might also want to untag any photos of the two of you.

Resist the urge to sneak peeks on his page through a mutual friend's account. Of course, you're only human and will be curious to know what he's up to, but you will only feel worse if you go on his page—kind of like Googling celebrity websites when you are in sweats with no makeup on and downing a pint of Häagen Dazs. Who needs that? Do you really need to see that he went boating with a pretty blonde a week after you split up on your birthday? We think not. Blocking is the essence of Next! With Facebook everyone has now become like a celebrity with public breakups—including the pain and humiliation of everyone seeing your relationship drama played out as if it were on a magazine cover.

Some might argue that blocking shows too much anger or resentment, but our feeling is that it's better to get an ex out of your life than to worry about what he and other people think. But if *you* broke up with him and are okay staying friends on Facebook, that's fine with us.

Amy, thirty-one, who broke so many *Rules* with her boy-friend that he dumped her, contacted us for advice about Face-book. We told her to de-friend and block her ex immediately so that she would stop looking at his page five times a day in hopes of getting information about who he was hooking up with and what he was doing. We told her to move on by post-ing a more glamorous default photo to replace the "funny face" one she had, and to write less about her day-to-day activities so she seemed more exciting and mysterious. Before consulting with us, she thought nothing of writing constant updates about the most mundane details of her day, including "going to yoga" or "snowed in..." or "any good eggnog reci-pes?" and/or complaining about her last relationship ("I hate men!"). We had her remove all such dreary or negative posts!

A month later Amy happily e-mailed us to say that her col-lege friend's older brother Matt had asked to be friends on Facebook. We told her to wait forty-eight hours, rather than her usual five minutes, to accept his request. He sent her a message immediately afterward saying, "You're really pretty! Thanks for the add. Maybe we can meet for drinks Tues-day night." We told her to wait four hours and then message him back, "Drinks would be great." She followed *The Rules* to the letter, ending their first date after one to two hours instead of her usual four or five.

Matt then messaged Amy the next day, on Saturday after-noon, about going out on a second date on Monday night. We told her not to respond that day or over the weekend, because all communication stops for a *Rules* Girl on the weekends—it's the dead zone. She waited until Sunday night and politely declined, determined to hold out for Saturday night date. He messaged her ten minutes later, "I'm totally free. How is Thursday, Friday or Saturday night?" Following *The Rules* Text-Back Times chart (see page 66), we told her to message him back three hours later: "Saturday night sounds great!"

By not responding so quickly to his messages, Amy avoided a flurry of interactions that would have made her seem too available and not that special. Instead, she was not an open book on Facebook and disappeared in between dates, which made him more interested and feel like he was dating a really sought-after girl!

After six consecutive Saturday night dates, Matt asked Amy to be exclusive. She said yes, but she did not change her relationship status or ask him to change his. We told her not to write on his wall or ask about his female friends on Facebook. She agreed, but wondered if she could post a photo of the two of them from an office party as her default photo now that they were exclusive. We told her not to, because it would be sending a possessive message to the world. Even though he initiated the relationship, posting such a public display of their relationship might make him feel smothered. Besides, if they broke up, she would have to take it down, which would be embarrassing and lead to lots of questions, so it was best to wait until he put a photo of them or changed his status to "in a relationship." Better still, she could even wait to put up a picture from their engagement photo shoot, or do it when she was adding his last name to her maiden name.

Amy confessed that she was not used to being so passive in a relationship, but agreed that the less aggressive or possessive she acted, the more Matt came after her. She also found that by being less into *the relationship* and by not posting about it, she had more time for her friends, family, career, and hobbies. When their two-year anniversary came up, her longest and best relationship ever, Matt surprised her with a ring.

Social networking sites are a great way to catch up with friends and stay current, but they can ruin a romantic relationship if used to bare all and make frequent contact with guys, and even with boyfriends. So keep guys wondering what you are up to and with who, where, and when...don't be an open book on Facebook!

Stay Away from His Facebook Profile

FACEBOOK CAN READ like a celebrity blog: who is breaking up with who or where, what couple is vacationing—lots of drama. The rumor mill updates as fast as your news feed these days, and it can be a lot to handle! Sometimes it's just TMI. While Facebook and other networking sites are great social outlets, they can cause a lot of confusion and misunderstanding. What you see, especially on a guy's profile, is not always what's really going on with him.

We understand that when you like a guy, you want to know everything about him. You want to walk by his house or office, you want to see what his ex-girlfriend looks like, you want to read his LinkedIn profile, his Twitter stream, or anything else for clues and insights into his personality. You want to study his Facebook profile like a religion. You want to see anything he's ever posted or was posted about him online. You want to spy on him!

But in doing so, you might notice things that irk you, like girls writing on his wall or tagging him in photos. You might find out about a party that you weren't invited to or see what he did Friday night that he didn't tell you about. What was that about the hot tub at the snowboarding event? Why is his arm around that girl? We understand it's upsetting to read or see these kinds of things, but that does not mean he is cheating or that you have anything to worry about. There are non-*Rules* Girls who will hug guys for the camera or try to make it seem like more is going on than there is. They have no life and want to find their fifteen minutes of fame on Facebook—don't give it to them! Don't believe everything you see or read. Sometimes a mean girl will post a photo of your crush with her just to stir things up. But don't freak out. Half the time it's not what you think!

Facebooking Gone Wrong

Cuddle up under a blanket and hug your teddy bear tight, because it's time for a true-life Facebook horror story: The future was looking bright for Jordan and Laura. After a few weeks of dating, Jordan made their relationship Facebook official, and even chose an adorable photo of the two of them for his new profile pic. Then things suddenly took a turn for the worse. It started small, with Laura typing a cutesy "Good morning!" post on Jordan's wall every day. Before long, though, she had filled his wall with lovey-dovey messages and romantic music videos that she had found on YouTube. Jordan's friends teased him mercilessly about it, and they even posted ultra-gushy comments on his wall blatantly mocking Laura's. After a while, it was all too much for Jordan to handle, and he decided to break things off—*via Facebook*. As if Laura wasn't embarrassed enough, dozens of Jordan's Facebook friends "liked" their breakup! Laura shouldn't have let her private feelings for Jordan become so public. Guys can be mushy, too, just not in such high doses—and not in plain sight of everyone they know.

—*Rules Daughters*

Pretend you were born in another era when all you knew about a guy was how he treated you, not what you might see on Facebook. You wouldn't write on his wall, much less be addicted to reading it. We know you're going to look at his profile, but here's the key: make sure you do not quote it when you are with him. Never even bring up his Facebook page, much less say, "I see Chelsea friended you" or "I guess you had a really busy day skiing." You will sound like a stalker.

Brooke, a junior in college, wrote to us saying that she was worried that her long-distance boyfriend in medical school was hooking up because she saw photos of him skiing with other girls on Facebook. It was a *Rules* relationship and they were exclusive, so we didn't think she had anything to worry about. We told Brooke not to bring it up with him. A few days later he said he was tired of not seeing her and booked a ticket for the weekend. Some guys just have female friends!

You need to go by a guy's actions, not what is posted on his wall. There are a lot of mean girls out there who will tag a guy in photos and write "had fun last night" or "hi cutie" on his wall just to cause trouble. You have to stay out of this silliness and not base your relationship on status updates.

Don't E-mail a Guy First and Keep It Brief (No E-books)!

MOST OF *THE RULES* that apply to texting apply to e-mailing. Never e-mail a guy first, keep it light and breezy, and wait to write back. But unlike texting, which is by necessity brief and to the point, e-mailing can be much more danger-ous. This medium lends itself to long-winded, diary-like dis-sertations. Some women are notorious for taking advantage of the blank screen—they can write up an entire e-book in one sitting and scare guys away! We have heard of some sending guys stanzas of their favorite poetry, passages from a novel they are reading, Myers-Briggs personality tests to find out if they are introverted or extroverted, links to news-worthy articles, relationship quizzes from *Cosmopolitan*, YouTube videos, chain letters that required forwarding to ten friends, and much more—and much worse! None of that is *Rules*-y at all!

This form of communication is great for BFFs, but is the kiss of death for a guy you are dating, especially in the first few months. Even if he asks a really open-ended question, like how things are going at work, treat it like a text mes-sage. Just write back, "Really productive week!" It's TMI to tell him that your assistant just quit, so you have a heavier workload and your project deadline has moved up three days and you are sure you have carpal tunnel syndrome from typing too much. (Um, maybe you should ease up on the long e-mails to him if your wrists hurt that much!)

Why E-mail at All?

A lot has changed since Tom Hanks and Meg Ryan fell in love via e-mail back in 1998's *You've Got Mail*. These days, e-mailing a guy you like is a level of awkward you just don't need to deal with. E-mail is fine for updating a long-distance boyfriend between Skype sessions, but no girl should be flirting with a potential prospect through an alias that ends with .com. On the off chance that your crush decides to e-mail you, you can definitely respond, but follow *The Rules* about when to write back and the length of your message. If he asks you how you're doing, resist the urge to update him on every insignificant aspect of your life, despite the blank screen begging for words to be typed. Before you do, though, you might want to ask yourself why this guy can't text or use Facebook like everyone else.

—*Rules Daughters*

We understand the temptation to write a lot. Being on your phone or laptop all the time, which many of us are, makes it easy to e-mail your guts out, especially on a slow workday, during a pit stop at Starbucks, or during a layover at an airport. But tell your girlfriends what's going on, not your crush or the guy you are dating. Long and/or frequent e-mails are a big turnoff. Few guys want to read paragraph after paragraph about a woman's feelings, thoughts, wants, or needs. A guy could feel obligated to stop whatever he is doing—studying, working, hanging out with the guys, watching a game—to write back. You don't want a guy to feel obligated to do anything. Furthermore, such e-mails will make it clear that you're the *opposite* of busy, and are spending your free time thinking about him!

We spoke to dozens of guys who said getting long and/ or frequent e-mails from women can be annoying. It's like a bad, drawn-out Ping-Pong match, with so much back-and-forth—"I couldn't get anything done when I was dating a big e-mailer. She wrote all day long," said one guy. Then he said he met a *Rules* Girl, who didn't e-mail him first and took half a day to write him back. "I found it refreshing. I don't want to communicate with my girlfriend all day. I want to get my work done and still be in a relationship. Is that asking too much?"

No, it's not! Girls, listen to what guys say, and don't e-mail first or frequently! As with any other form of communication, e-mailing improperly is aggressive and intrusive, so don't do it no matter what interesting tidbits you feel like sharing, whether it's a YouTube clip of a great new song or the menu from that new Italian restaurant you want to try. Such e-mails are obvious cries for attention ("Think of me! Remember me!") and flirting—nothing a *Rules* Girl would ever do! *Rules* Girls don't need to ask for attention; they naturally get it by being busy—too busy to e-mail guys.

Not only shouldn't you e-mail first, but you need to wait at least four hours to e-mail him back the first time and anywhere from thirty minutes to three hours to answer subsequent ones, just like with text messages (see *Rule* #6 again). The weekends (Friday 6 p.m. to Sunday 6 p.m.) are still a dead zone, as you want to give guys the impression you are out and about, not sitting around at your computer. The only time you can respond to a weekend e-mail is if it's a scheduling thing—for example, if you already have a date in place and he wants to pick you up at 7 p.m. instead of 8 p.m. to take you to a karaoke bar before dinner and asks if that is okay. You can wait thirty minutes and write back something as simple as "Sure." Remember, you can talk on the date!

With clients who do online dating we suggest that they keep their answers to guys' e-mails brief and light and breezy. No matter that he e-mailed you his whole life story, including what happened in his last three relationships and his political and religious beliefs, because it could be a form letter he wrote to thirty other women that says nothing specific about you or anyone else. Just e-mail back, "Hi, you sound interesting." When he asks you out, you can talk on the date about all his interests and his life story.

If a guy you met online or through a friend is trying to set up a first date, but keeps changing the date or the plans, write back very little, as you don't want to encourage a time waster. We had one client who got an e-mail from a guy she hadn't met yet explaining why he had to reschedule their first drink date. "Sorry to have to postpone our first date. Just got back from a business trip to LA. Again my apologies, but I am definitely going to make this happen soon." She wanted to e-mail him back five minutes later, "Welcome back from LA. How was the weather? Totally understand. Let's definitely get something on the calendar after Easter break." Too much! We told her to write back three days later (not one day later because he had canceled previously): "No problem!"

The e-mail that requires the briefest response is a breakup e-mail. If a guy has the gall to end your relationship in this heartless way, just write back, "No worries!" Don't journal about how hurt you are and how you didn't see it coming and what he did wrong, you did wrong, or you both did wrong. Any guy who would end a relationship by e-mail is not looking for—or deserving of—closing commentary. Next!

E-mail does have its advantages and appropriate uses. It's less personal than a phone call, which can work in your favor. If a guy you are dating leaves a message on your cell, e-mail him back. We don't encourage calling, because you might catch him at a bad time, whereas e-mail is never intrusive. Besides, it's always a better conversation when he calls you because you know he is in the mood to talk. So we tell clients to just write, "Hey, just getting back to you. Crazy busy day!" and let him call again. Remember, you want e-mails and calls leading to dates—not to more e-mails!

Make Yourself Invisible and Other Ways to Get Out of Instant Messaging

INSTANT MESSAGING MAKES doing *The Rules* so much harder. How can you make a guy wait to see you or even speak to you so he appreciates you when you're literally available online for talking to? Instant messaging is like running into a guy on a street corner or at the water cooler at work and chatting for an hour. How hard to get are you when a guy can chat you up and know you are available that second? Don't you have somewhere to go or something to do? Or can you pretend you do?

Even if you have nothing going on, you cannot let a guy know that by IMing him back in nanoseconds. As with any other form of communication, a guy should have to wait to hear from you. For a guy to stay intrigued, there has to be a little bit of a bungee jump for him. Don't take that away by IMing him back right away and chatting for an hour or more!

We know that guys can be relentless when they like you and want to know everything about you. They like to catch you online and get in your face. They fire away questions as if you were on *Jeopardy*, *Who Wants to Be a Millionaire?*, or some other quiz show. It's like a rapid-fire interrogation: "Hey, what's up? How was your weekend?" Then, ten minutes later when you say you have to run: "Why do you have to get off now? Where are you going? What's the rush? I thought your trainer was at 3 p.m. It's only 2. What else is going on? I don't see you on instant messaging anymore. Are you blocking me? What's going on? You're so hard to reach…" Giving a guy online time doesn't always lead to dates. Women are catching on to this poor excuse for a date: Lynnie, twenty-five, a software sales rep, told us she is tired of chatting with a guy online for an hour or more, feeling close, and then nothing coming of it. Sometimes you get lucky and the guy asks you out, but he also tries to monopolize your time with constant IMs, making it hard to follow the don't-talk-to-him-24/7 *Rule*. But if you let him get too much too soon from you electronically, he might eventually get bored.

The problem is that we are all available all the time—but you can't let him catch you online all the time! If you answer every chat, you will no longer be the mysterious, hard-to-get girl who is busy dating other guys, but instead the girl who is glued to her computer. But how can you avoid letting him know you're available when in reality you *are* sitting at your desk or on your laptop in class all day or doing research online in the evening?

One way to do so is to make yourself appear "invisible." That way, you won't show up on his chat list—or on anyone else's. If you see someone you want to chat with (like your mom or your BFF), you can initiate the IM without anyone bothering you. Another option is to set your status to "busy" or "unavailable." This will show up on his chat list and it will discourage him from contacting you, or give you an automatic reason not to respond at all if he does. But don't be too obvious by changing your status once he has already

Status Messages and Away Messages

As you've probably figured out by now, you don't have to be face-to-face with—or even talking to—a guy to send the wrong message. Even if you aren't in the middle of an IM chat, your away message and/or status might still be working against you. Any girl out of school should know better than to post an angsty Taylor Swift lyric as part of her IM auto-reply, but not every girl realizes what qualifies as an acceptable away message otherwise. The short answer: none. Just sign off! There's no need to stay online only to announce that you're not at the computer. The same basic *Rule* applies to all instant messenger statuses: just don't post any. If you want to use your status to publicize a fund-raiser you're helping with or an upcoming event once in a while, no one will hold it against you, but resist the urge to keep everyone up-to-date on your latest thoughts and feelings. That just makes it seem like you spend your life glued to your IM—and you should remain a bit mysterious. Give the guys on your buddy list the impression that you have better ways to spend your time, whether or not that's true. If they're left wondering where you are and what you're up to, who knows? They just may send you a text to find out.

—*Rules Daughters*

sent you an IM! In some forms of IM, you can also block a guy by going into your privacy settings. But be aware that he can ask someone else to check if you are online or even create another screen name and find out you are purposely hiding from him—use this method with caution!

If you know you are someone who can't resist temptation,

then you should just sign out of chat. Exit the program, or turn off instant messaging. You can be on these websites without everyone knowing it and without being so readily available. If he tries to chat when you are offline (or at least *appear* offline), the IM will turn into a message or e-mail, which you can just answer later according to *The Rules* timetable.

But if you don't want to or can't do one of the above, then you need to get out of there. You can learn how to end IM chats quickly—in ten minutes or less. When we tell women to do this, they are shocked. They argue that it's rude and that they are way too nice to cut off a chat in ten minutes. What if the guy is in the middle of saying something important? We invariably find that such women are people-pleasers who also have a hard time getting off the phone with chatterbox friends or just saying no in general. We tell them "nice" is giving to charity or helping out at a shelter, but that it's people-pleasing and being a doormat to stay on an IM chat for an hour—it's better to get off abruptly than let a guy chat you up and not ask you out!

Here are some good conversation enders to prevent long IMs:

"I have to run!" *Then log off before the guy has a chance to ask where you are going and what you are doing. It's none of his business. If he wants to know all about you, let him e-mail or text or call you for a date. An IM chat is not a date!*

"My Pilates class starts soon—have to go get ready."

"So sorry, I have to hop on this call…"

"I'm meeting a friend for coffee…and I'm already late!"

"My internet is acting funny."

"The program keeps signing me out!"

"My boss needs me..."

You get the idea! Say whatever you have to and just shut it down. Remember, you have a life—college, work, friends, hobbies, the gym, and hopefully dates—so you really don't have more than ten minutes to chat. Set a timer if you have to. If a guy has so much to say and so much to ask you, he can do it on a date!

Rule #13

Don't Talk Too Much in the First Few Weeks

WOMEN ARE OFTEN insulted when we tell them not to spill too much on the first few dates or in texts or in general. They argue, "But how will he get to know me? How will he find out how smart or funny I am? More importantly, how will we get close?" And with all the latest technology at their disposal, they have even more ways to talk to guys and break *The Rules* than ever before! Our answer is always: *slowly!* In the first week, a new guy should know only a few facts about you, like where you go to college, or work, and what you like to do for fun. As the relationship progresses, you can tell him a little bit more about yourself, like tidbits about your family and friends. He should be asking you a lot of questions to get you to talk, not getting bored by long stories. Giving him too much information shows that you are eager or nervous—and perhaps have not been on many dates lately!

If you want to bond with a guy, talk and text less and laugh and listen more. The less you talk, the more he will open up and the more he will wonder what you are thinking about. Everyone loves a good listener. Besides, guys are used to having their ears chewed off by women! He'll be pleasantly surprised if you are not a chatterbox or a marathon texter or Facebook junkie…at any age!

The best way to make sure you don't overshare is to keep the dates short—see *Rule #7*. If you are going on marathon dates (drinks, more drinks at another bar, dinner, dessert, movie, party, club), you are more likely to tell your whole life story. Another way to avoid talking too much is not to drink or to have only one alcoholic beverage. When you have two or more drinks or start to get tipsy, you will often say (and do) more than you want to and even embarrass yourself, but we'll get to that in *Rule #21*.

You might think we are asking you to be superficial, but anything is better than baring your soul. Many women make the mistake of telling way too much way too soon, as if the date were a therapy session, thinking they will bond over these revelations. But in the beginning, a guy isn't even your friend yet. Until you have been seeing each other for a few months and he has said he likes you a lot and you are exclusive, your childhood and innermost feelings are none of his business. Even then, keep diary-type stuff to yourself or to your girlfriends!

When you do interact, whether by text, on a date, or otherwise, there is much to stay away from, too. Do not bring up words like "love," "marriage," "engagement," "wedding," or "babies." Don't tell him that you just watched *The Notebook* for the fifteenth time. Do not tell or text him that your twin sister is getting married and you are looking for a date to the wedding. Do not text him that your other sister is pregnant with a girl and you can't wait to have a niece. Do not message him on Facebook that your younger brother is in rehab, so you are busy next weekend with family visiting day. Do not tell or text him that your parents got divorced when you were five and you do not really talk to or see that much of your dad, who left your mom for a younger woman. Do not tell or text him that you are still paying off your college loans and are just making ends meet and that's why you can't split the bill. Besides, the reason you don't split the bill is because you are a *Rules* Girl and it is his pleasure to take you out and pay! More on that later. Dating is not an open forum! Ditto for using information from his Facebook page to make conversation on dates. Doing so will put you in the category of social networking stalker, as we said in *Rule #9*.

Don't tell him anything unflattering in any area of your life, like that you flunked physics or that your parents pulled strings to get you your job. Do not tell him you had a fight with your roommate and had to sleep somewhere else. We are not telling you to lie and say you went to Harvard if you didn't, but you don't have to volunteer bad stuff. It's none of his business.

Do not share any childhood traumas or tell him that you are in therapy or that you see a life coach. In other words, do not get too deep too soon. Intensity will scare a guy away in the early months of dating.

Do not tell him all about your past relationships and what went wrong and what you are looking for now. Do not tell him when or how you lost your virginity or that your ex cheated on you or anything negative about your dating life. Some women think that dating is truth serum and text or message a guy on Facebook that they haven't had a boyfriend or sex in three years. TMI! We said not to talk too much on dates—we didn't say not to think! Once your personal life is out there, especially in writing, it can't be taken back.

Also, don't fill in lulls in the conversation. Trying to fill in the silences reeks of desperation and shows that you are trying too hard. Making jokes or trying to entertain him with funny stories and anecdotes shows too much interest. You don't want him to know how much you care about him or think that you are the funny girl instead of the intriguing girl. Remember, sometimes when there is silence, it's because he's thinking how pretty you are when your fringe falls into your eyes or even imagining what you look like naked.

In the beginning, a guy might give you the impression that he loves to talk and e-mail and text a lot, too. He might go along with three-hour Skype chats and marathon textfests and Facebook chats that go into the middle of the night, and you will convince yourself that this guy is different from other guys and actually likes to talk. But you will be wrong. One day he will dump you and block you on Facebook and you will have no idea why—but we do. You interacted or talked too much in the first few weeks!

Allie, a twenty-three-year-old graduate student in Middle Eastern studies, met Ori, a cute Israeli resident, on a work-study program. He spoke to her first, and in just a matter of weeks, their relationship became fast and furious. Many nights they talked until 2 a.m. about politics and science. They hung out in coffee shops for hours and she said they had "amazing sex." After two months of dating, he said, "Let's keep in touch" and even suggested she visit him again during her winter break. Allie interpreted this sudden togetherness as true love. So when she flew back to Boston, she didn't think twice about texting him and e-mailing him and chatting with him on Facebook.

Allie confidently thought, "This is great. I can talk to him whenever I want about whatever I want. Maybe I will move to Israel one day." They Skyped for hours and exchanged long, loving e-mails. He asked her what her favorite flower was, they wrote each other poems, and she e-mailed him articles and endearing texts that started with "Happy Monday!" She even Evited him to her birthday party and when he couldn't make it, she said, "No worries, I will FaceTime you in." She wrote on his wall, "You make me happy!"

Two weeks after Allie returned, Ori began answering fewer and fewer texts. Then one day Allie stopped hearing from him altogether. She got his voice mail every time she called. He wasn't returning her e-mails. She couldn't find him on Facebook and got worried. She thought maybe he had taken his account down, but then she called her BFF to check and found out his profile was still up—he had blocked her! Allie was in shock when she called us. She couldn't believe that what was a soul connection for her was just a fling for him. We told her that had she not talked to him so much through so many different technologies, she would have found out sooner that he was not that interested. Or, had she followed *The Rules* and disappeared, he would have been more into her. When you act aloof in the beginning about a guy who initially likes you, he starts to pick up the pace: "Hey, are you okay? Are we okay? What are you up to? What are you doing for winter break? I have two weeks off and frequent-flier miles."

The lesson here? Being available 24/7 can be the kiss of death. We told Allie what we tell all our clients: when you meet your soul mate, get really busy in between dates and keep the conversation light and breezy. If a guy says, "What's your favorite food?" you can say, "Sushi, what about you?" to be polite and find out more about him. But don't ask anything serious, like "Why did you and your last girlfriend break up?" or "Where do you see yourself after grad school?" It is too clear that you like him and want to know about his past and future and where you might fit into it.

Less is always more with men! You can talk and text your

guts out to your girlfriends, your therapist, your life coach, even a coworker or stranger at the gym, but you can't talk, text, tweet, e-mail, or otherwise interact with a guy too much without overwhelming him and possibly driving him away. If you want a guy to miss and pursue you, disappear in between dates!

Don't Just Hang Out or See Him 24/7

THE SIMPLE ACT of hanging out has become more popu-
lar in recent years, as it, too, is part of our increasingly casual
culture. Perhaps a guy and girl will text back and forth for
a while and then agree to meet at the same bar or party an
hour or so later just to hang out. The next time they will hang
out again or hang out and hook up. This may go on for weeks
or months or years. They may never go out on a dinner date
or become boyfriend and girlfriend. This kind of casual non-
dating is especially common in college.

Just hanging out might be okay for girls who don't really
care about dates or serious relationships, but it is not okay for
Rules Girls. *Rules* Girls get asked out several days in advance.
Hanging out requires little or no effort on the guy's part and
is therefore a big nothing—so don't be flattered by it. If he
always texts you at 6 p.m., "Do you want to hang out later?"
you need to start responding, "Sorry, but I already have
plans," even if you don't have plans and even if you really like
him—especially if you really like him! You must hold out for
a real date, or at least *some* advance plan!

You might be thinking that this *Rule* is disingenuous and
game-playing, but it is really about having a life, being busy,

and setting the bar high so a guy respects you. If you agree to hang out on just a few hours' notice, then you will become the last-minute girl—not the girl he makes restaurant reservations for. Remember, a guy will try to get away with the least possible effort whenever he can. He may try to see you only when he is bored or his original plans fell through. Don't be his plan B. You must silently show a guy that he has to work to get you by saying no to spur-of-the-moment hanging out.

Jackie, a college freshman, told us that amid everyone hanging out and hooking up around Frat Row, there was one sophomore girl in her dorm who always turned down last-minute or casual offers. Now she is the only girl in her pledge class with a boyfriend! "There was just something about her that made him want to take her out on dates," Jackie wrote to us. Exactly. *The Rules!*

Another way to give a guy the wrong idea is to see him too much, especially in the first few crucial months. Most guys come on strong in the beginning. If they like you, they want to see you every day if you let them, because the more they see you, the faster they get to know you—and the faster you'll have sex perhaps. But if you agree to see them every day, they *will* eventually get bored and start asking for space. They will say things like "I'm not looking for anything serious right now" or "Work is really busy" and cancel on you, even though it was *their* idea to see you all the time! They may start asking other women out because you have ceased being a challenge. We have seen this scenario many times. Familiarity breeds contempt, while absence makes the heart grow fonder. Don't be seduced by guys who try to see you all the time or who get angry if you say no. If a guy really wants to see you seven days a week, he'll have to propose to you!

Here's the tricky thing, though. Even though he's the one asking you out, you can't expect a guy to pace the relationship—you have to be the one to do it. This means saying no to whirlwind courtships. These relationships start out fast and furious and ultimately end the same way, like a train wreck. Just look at Hollywood: how many couples have we seen "connect" on a movie set or at a party and become inseparable, only to break up a few months later? Seeing a guy every day in the first three months is sheer lunacy, whether you are a movie star or a waitress. A *Rules*-y star would be too busy with other auditions and starlet friends to accept dates 24/7, so the guy experiences longing, as opposed to familiarity followed by boredom. Remember, less is more with men! Besides, there is no way to know what a guy is *really* like in so short a time.

Pacing a relationship means seeing him once or twice a week for the first month and no more than four or five times a week when you are in a committed, exclusive relationship, which he will hopefully take to the next level with a ring! We realize such self-restraint can be difficult, because when you are dating a guy you really like you want to see him as much as possible. You want to know everything about him and get close physically and emotionally. You may want to cancel plans with friends, stop going to the gym, skip studying, or take a day off work just to be with him. The last thing you want to do is to tell him you can't go out with him, especially if you haven't met anyone you really like in a while. *But you must!* Give him the impression that your life is full, that it existed before him and still exists now. You should never make a guy that important; he is a part of your life, not your whole life. You should continue to be a friend, a student, a worker, a daughter, a sister, or whatever you were before you met him. Besides, you're not just hanging out anyway! How many dates can you really plan in a week? Limiting how much you see him, even if you have nothing else going on, is good not only for the relationship, but for you, too. It will force you to find things to do, like join a book club or take up yoga, or tennis.

Rachel, twenty-six, was getting her MBA when she met her future boyfriend at a party. She thought he was really cute and almost fainted when he asked her out. But she was in a two-week training program and couldn't see him right away. In the past, Rachel had made guys more important than her school work and regretted it. Although she was afraid it might make him move on to another girl, she told him she was busy for the next two weeks. He said, "You must have a lot of dates. Don't forget me!" She just laughed, neither confirming nor denying. He called her two weeks later to the day—and he still teases Rachel now about how she made him wait so long!

Rachel's story proves that when you turn guys down, they don't think that you are rude or lying or playing a game—they think you are popular and busy with other guys! Volunteering information ("I'm working on my MBA and can't see you right now") too soon is neither necessary nor flattering. When a guy likes you and you are a challenge, his imagination is always more interesting than whatever you may really be doing!

Now, let's say you and the guy you are dating go to the same college or live in the same apartment building or work at the same company. How do you maintain mystery and separate yourself when you can conceivably run into each other *all* the time? We suggest trying to avoid him occasionally! Take a different route to class or go to another coffee shop.

If you always run into each other in the kitchen at 11:30, start going at 10:45 instead. Have a girls' night out or stay in to study. Create as much courtship and structure for the relationship as possible. College is an intrinsically casual environment, so you might even pretend you go to different schools so you have your own life.

Are Groups Ever *Appropriate?*

"Just hanging out" might not be ideal for a girl trying to land herself a boyfriend, but group hangouts account for at least half, if not more, of the social life of any college student. If you're sitting with friends in a lounge watching a movie or out at the local bar, you can't really control whether your crush drops by and joins in, and making constant excuses to duck out might lose you some friends (or possibly even raise some eyebrows about nasty bathroom troubles). In such situations, it's best to just stay put and act natural. Be sure not to stare or keep glancing over at him too much; you don't want to come off as desperate—or worse, as a stalker. Have a good time as if he's not even there, by talking and laughing with your friends. You want to seem like the coolest girl in the room, the one he'll want to approach and talk to himself. If and when he does, let it progress naturally from there. If he hasn't asked you out already, a group hangout might just turn out to be the perfect opportunity to lay the foundation for something more. Then it won't be long before you're *both* leaving the rest of the group behind for some one-on-one time.

—*Rules Daughters*

Juliana, twenty-nine, recently e-mailed us to say that the guy she has been dating for three months is head over heels with her and she attributes it to this *Rule*. They met on Match.com and after three e-mail exchanges, he asked her out for drinks. They hit it off and he texted her the next day, "Hey gorgeous, any chance I can take you out to dinner tonight or one night this week?" Juliana was unemployed and had absolutely nothing going on that night or any night that week. But she was determined to do *The Rules* and said she was "crazy busy all week." So he asked Juliana out for the following Saturday night and she accepted. After their third-consecutive Saturday night date, he asked her, "Is it too early to get serious? I don't want to share you with anyone else." Because Juliana had turned him down a lot, he assumed she had dates and asked to be exclusive. When he introduces her to friends today, he still says, "This is the girl I told you about who wouldn't see me."

We have spoken to couples who have been married for decades. The husbands who seem the craziest about their wives never forget how the women refused to hang out or see them more often, whether by design or accident. Steven remembers chatting up his future wife, Alice, at a mutual friend's party and how she wouldn't give him the time of day. Truth be told, Alice was recently divorced and shy about dating again. She had also heard that he was a player, so when he approached her she immediately told him she was "divorced with a young child" so he wouldn't waste her time. He said, "I thought we could hang out sometime." She clearly told him, "I don't hang out." He said, "Then let me take you out for dinner." She accepted. He proposed after a year and they just celebrated their thirtieth anniversary. Alice wasn't exactly following *The Rules* (there was no book back then); she was just being cautious. Of course, her caution turned a player into a devoted husband and father. "Honestly, I couldn't get rid of him!" she said.

Remember, courtship is not casual!

Rule #15

Let Him Suggest Skype and Visit You More in a Long-Distance Relationship

THESE DAYS, YOU can be in a long-distance relationship and literally never be with the guy you are dating. There are so many ways to video chat now: Skype, FaceTime, and probably many more ways that hadn't even been invented yet when this book went to press. But video chat does not make a relationship! Skype and FaceTime are glorified phone calls—they are *not* dates. The guy is not taking you out to dinner or really doing anything. His efforts are next to nothing! Don't be flattered if a guy wants to video chat every day for hours. He may just be bored or lonely. Unless he comes to see you—whether by plane, train, or automobile—every other week, he either has a girlfriend or is just not that interested. If it's a semester-abroad situation or you live in different countries, that's a different story—but more about that from our daughters!

If you are confused as to whether you are in a *Rules*-y long-distance relationship, pretend you live in the 1980s. Before any kind of video-based technology existed, a guy would have to travel to see you. We already know that too much technology is not always a good thing. Don't be so quick to agree to long Skype sessions morning, noon, and night and decline FaceTime invitations sometimes so you are

Study Abroad

For college girls, study abroad puts a new spin on the standard long-distance relationship, and as a result it comes with a very specific set of *Rules*. Unlike other LDRs, study-abroad relationships have a not-too-distant end in sight, usually a semester or summer apart. It can be tough when you leave your guy behind or he heads off to spend a few months in some exotic locale—especially if his destination has a reputation for romance and dark-eyed beauties—but in these situations, the best way to hold on to your boyfriend is actually to let go of him a little bit.

It's common for some guys to suggest taking a break from the relationship while one or both of you are out exploring another country, so don't panic if this happens to you. While a relationship break might be a sign of the end under normal circumstances, the *Rules* of study abroad are just a little different. These guys often convince themselves that a break is best to get the most out of their time apart from you, but don't bust out your box of tissues just yet. Play it cool and go along with it. If he really cares about you, there's *no way* he'll be able to go without you for a full four months—he'll be texting and suggesting Skype dates long before anyone starts packing for their return flight. And if he doesn't? Well, we're sorry to say, in that case it's time for you to find a dark-eyed beauty of your own.

—*Rules Daughters*

not always accessible. When you do accept a video chat, end it after twenty minutes—you don't have time to sit around! Not only should you take these actions, but you should also never initiate them, just like with every other form of communication. Initiating a video chat is even *worse* than texting or calling because you must be sitting at your computer. How are you going to do that if you're out living a full, busy life?

A long-distance relationship should not stay that way for long stretches of time. He should be figuring out when to see you and how you can be together, whether that means his relocating or your relocating—but the latter will happen only after he proposes with a ring and you set a wedding date. In a *Rules* relationship, the guy wants to breathe the same air as you; he never wants to be apart for too long. As we said in our first book, he must visit you three times in a long-distance relationship before you visit him. It may sound funny to say, but the situation should not be equal. If the guy you are dating is making excuses as to why he can't visit you every week or month, it's not a long-distance relationship—it's a fantasy relationship, courtesy of the internet and video chatting. We know. We hear the war stories.

Erica, a thirty-year-old gallery owner, met Max, a thirty-five-year-old teacher's assistant, at the Louvre in Paris. They were both staring at the *Mona Lisa* when Max said, "It's smaller than you thought, right? Where are you from? I'm from Chicago." Erica laughed and told Max she was from Washington, DC. They hit it off and Max asked Erica if she wanted to get coffee and croissants at a nearby café. Erica said, "Pourquoi pas?" They talked nonstop for three hours. Erica could not believe how much they had in common. They soon realized they were both leaving Paris the next morning, so they decided to meet up for dinner as well. After splitting a bottle of wine, Erica ended up staying at Max's hotel room; they had sex that night and again in the morning. They shared a cab to the airport. They talked about art, philosophy, religion, and history effortlessly, as if they had known each other for years—not just one day. They finished each other's sentences.

When they got back to the States, Max was texting and e-mailing Erica all day, every day. "I dreamt about you last night, I will write you a poem. Who is your favorite poet?" She wrote him back with equal frequency and gusto. They began to Skype at crazy hours and Erica started skipping her morning cardio classes to be available to Max, who liked to chat early in the day. Erica updated her Facebook status: "I think I found love in the city of light!"

Despite the flurry of texts, e-mails, Facebook messages, and Skype sessions for two months, Max never mentioned meeting up again. Erica was so flattered by the constant contact that she did not notice (or pretended not to notice) the obvious, until her *Rules*-minded friend said, "If this guy is so crazy about you, why isn't he visiting you?" Erica blamed it on Max's busy schedule. Nonetheless, she decided to invite him to DC to a gallery opening to "move things along." Max said he would love to come but was tied up with work. Erica did not want to let another two months go by and remembered that she had a friend on Facebook in Chicago she could reconnect with as a pretext to see Max. Max seemed thrilled, but said that his car was being serviced so he would not be able to pick her up from the airport. He invited her to stay with him and said he would take her out to dinner. Erica was as excited as a schoolgirl about the prospect of spending a few days with Max and becoming closer, but she should not have been. After all, how much effort does it take for a guy to let you stay at his place in exchange for sex and companionship? Very little!

While their reunion was nice, Erica noticed that it was not nearly as romantic as their texts and e-mails and video chats. Max's phone beeped constantly and it seemed as if he was juggling her into his busy schedule, not making her a priority. When Erica left, she felt empty and disappointed. She decided to call her *Rules*-y friend, who gave her a copy of the book and suggested she call us for a consultation. We went over the whole relationship from the moment they met to the present. Erica forwarded us all their texts and e-mails to see if we could salvage the relationship. We nicely told Erica all the mistakes she had made from day one: spending more than twenty minutes with Max when they first met, sleeping with him too soon, baring her soul on Skype, and visiting him first. Not only was the relationship a case of too much, too soon, but Erica was the only one keeping it alive. Because she had been so easy to get, Max didn't feel that she was special. Max was happy to chat with her online or to see her when she visited him, but he was not going out of his way to see her. He might have even been dating one of his students—Erica was his pen pal/hookup buddy—for all she knew. Erica agreed to distance herself from Max and put *The Rules* into practice.

Erica suddenly became very busy with work and the gym and her friends. She also joined Match.com, as she and Max were hardly exclusive, despite their many deep talks. She ignored his texts if they weren't about visiting her—and they weren't. We told her to sign out of Skype so he could not reach her spontaneously and would have to e-mail her to schedule a video chat instead. We told her to limit these sessions to once a week for twenty minutes and to go back to her morning cardio classes. If Max wanted to see her pretty face, he would have to hop on a plane to DC. No more long e-mails or texts about poetry and religion, just "swamped at the gallery." In response to questions like "What are you up to?" she wrote, "At the gym, can't talk" or "at movies with friends...got2go!" For all of Max's musings about poetry and life, he had never said *anything* about getting together with her.

After a week of *Rules* boot camp, Max noticed that Erica was less available and sent her some texts asking her what she was up to and if she planned to be in Chicago again, but he said nothing about visiting her. Fortunately, she had met a guy who lived nearby in Virginia on Match.com, who took her out on a real date, which helped her get over Max quickly. She realized, thanks to *The Rules*, that the long-distance relationship she was in was not really a relationship at all.

In some cases, a client will insist that she followed the long-distance *Rules*, specifically that she waited to visit him after he had visited her three times, but wonders why the relationship still did not work out. When we review her situation in a consultation, we find out that after his third visit, she threw *The Rules* out the window. It's important to remember that even once you reach that three-visit threshold, it's still about letting him pursue you. It's about dating a guy who doesn't want to be apart from you. A woman must follow the spirit of *The Rules*, not just the fine print.

Sophie, thirty-four, a New Yorker, met Jordan, thirty-seven, at a happy hour near her office on a Friday night. Jordan had flown in from Seattle for a real estate conference and was leaving the next morning. He walked up to Sophie and asked her if he could buy her a drink. They talked about work, weather, and travel. After twenty minutes, Jordan asked if she wanted to have dinner, but Sophie declined. In the past she had rationalized spending five hours with out-of-town guys because they were leaving the next day, but she had read *The Rules* and knew that was a big mistake.

Jordan took Sophie's number and said he would be in touch soon. The next day he texted her from JFK airport to say that he had a great time and would love to see her again. He asked if she had any plans to be in Seattle and she wrote back, "No, can't get away anytime soon." Jordan wrote back, "Well, if the only way I can see you again is to fly to New York, so be it." He booked a flight two weeks later and took Sophie to dinner and on a horse-and-buggy ride around Central Park. Jordan asked if he could stay at her apartment but, following *The Rules*, she said, "Sorry, I'm not comfortable with that yet, but I can recommend a great hotel." Two weeks later, Jordan had another work conference in New York and took Sophie out to dinner and a show. She let him sleep over, but on the couch—no sex. Again, Jordan asked if Sophie would consider coming to Seattle and said he would even pay for the plane ticket. She wrote back, "I just can't take time off from work right now." Jordan had a college reunion coming up in New Jersey a month later, so he wrote, "No problem, I will swing by and see you then."

So far, so good! In between visits, Jordan initiated texts, e-mails, and FaceTime chats. For their third date, Jordan booked a hotel room in the city and took Sophie to dinner, drinking and dancing. They stayed out until 4 a.m. and ended up sleeping together. After cuddling all morning and having breakfast in bed, Sophie started to feel like she was falling for the tall, handsome realtor.

Now that Jordan had met the three-visit quota, Sophie felt she could show more initiative. So when he asked again if she could come to Seattle for a weekend, she excitedly responded, "Let me see what I can do." An hour later, she friended a college roommate on Facebook who had moved to Seattle to say she was going to be in her area and ask if she wanted to go on a double date. She begged her boss to let her take off a week for a family emergency and then called the airline to use her frequent-flier miles. She then e-mailed Jordan that "actually I can be in Seattle after all. I have a lot of vacation time." Jordan was taken aback but texted her, "Wow, that sounds great!"

As often happens when a woman starts making moves like these, even in a *Rules* relationship, Sophie went overboard and set herself up for disappointment. She asked Jordan if he could pick her up from the airport, and he said he would love to but had client meetings back to back—could she call her friend or take a cab? Then, instead of showering her with dinners and a romantic tour of the city, Jordan worked late, ordered in Chinese takeout, and then fell asleep after sex. When Sophie asked if he could show her the town, he suggested she go with her friend because he had to work late. When she asked for a drawer to put her things in, he gave her an empty shopping bag. Ouch!

After Sophie left, Jordan said nothing specific about meeting again. He rather casually texted, "I guess I'll see you the next time I'm in New York for work." Hurt and confused, Sophie decided to throw a New Year's party and sent Jordan an Evite. First he texted, "will try, sounds like fun!" and then a week later he wrote, "hard to get flights over the holiday, sorry babe." The next day Sophie saw photos of Jordan with other women on his Facebook page and realized that she had not been a serious relationship for him. She decided to confront Jordan on iChat to ask him if it was just a fling, as she was seriously thinking about relocating to Seattle if he thought they had a future. "I think you're pretty and sweet, but you're a New Yorker and I'm a Seattle guy. We're very different people. Honestly, I don't think this is going to work."

Sophie learned the hard way that even if a guy visits you first and does so three times, that doesn't necessarily mean it's serious. Jordan was not always in New York for Sophie, but for fun, for work, and for a college reunion. Also, if he invites you to visit him for a weekend, don't go for a week, even if you have vacation time, a friend in his city, and frequent-flier miles. Like Jordan, he will feel overwhelmed by so much sudden togetherness and interest. For it to be a *Rules* long-distance relationship, *he* has to figure out how to spend more time with you in your city. He has to say he wants to be exclusive, say "I love you," and plot how to be together, whatever it takes.

A woman can come up with the craziest reasons for traveling to a guy first! She rationalizes it by saying she doesn't want him to see that she still lives with her parents or is embarrassed about her crappy studio apartment. We tell her to get over it. A guy who likes you won't care if you live at home or in a hovel, but traveling to him will make you seem desperate and not busy. Don't do it! The most common temptation is free airfare or miles. Even if a guy offers to pay for you to fly to him or sends a limo for the first few dates, don't go. It's not about the money, it's about the effort. He should be the one to pack a suitcase and be inconvenienced, otherwise how will you know that he really likes you? You are not a call girl who can be bought with a car service. We know women who sign up for millionaire dating services and the guys refuse to leave their duplexes or mansions. They want to pay for the women to travel to them. A *Rules* Girl says, "No, thanks." If he can't get away to see you, you can't get away either! He's not more important than you, even if he is a CEO and you are a secretary! We don't care if you have a cousin in his city or just want to get the heck out of town—*The Rules* are more important. If you travel to him for any reason, he will cease having to work hard to see you. Think long-term gratification, not short-term fun!

When it's a *Rules* long-distance relationship, a guy just can't take that you are not together. He drives three hours or hops on a plane every week or two; he searches for a college or a job in your city; he relocates; he proposes. He doesn't let too much time go by, because it's painful not being with you. There is not a lot of arguing about who is going to visit whom. You don't have to put a gun to his head to make him come see you. Remember that guys travel hours for football games and concerts. He might joke, "Are you ever going to visit me?" but when you giggle and say, "I really don't like driving long distances or at night," he'll come to you. It's a given that the guy is going to do the legwork.

Rule #16 ——————————————————————————

Don't Lose Your Friends Because You're So Obsessed with a Guy!

W OMEN WHO BREAK *The Rules* with guys do not make the best girlfriends. They are usually so busy texting or talking about the guy that they either ignore their friends or bore them to death. And if they have a crush on a guy who isn't even interested in them, they become delusional and expect their friends to lie to them as well. Have you ever been with a friend who was in the middle of a textfest or instant-message chat with a guy? You feel like you're with a zombie! She is physically with you, but mentally a million miles away. If you are a *Rules* Girl, you try to nicely nudge her to get off the phone for her own sake (and yours!) but she totally ignores you, or holds up her index finger to signal one more minute or mouths, "Hold on." But then another ten minutes go by and then twenty or thirty. It's frustrating, to say the least. If you left the room, she would hardly notice or miss you. She's obsessed!

Of course, girls who do *The Rules* aren't this kind of friend. They end texting chats quickly. They don't dump girlfriends for a last-minute date or hookup. They don't force roommates to endure a guy sleeping in their room every night. They don't flirt with their friend's crush. They *do* have boundaries and self-respect!

As you know by now, it's a good thing for a guy to see that you are too busy to be thinking about him and contacting him constantly. Well, what are you so busy with all this time? Your girlfriends! You have a full life with training sessions, shopping trips, and dinners! Maybe you get together with *Rules*-minded friends and meet every week for coffee or Chinese food (like we used to!) and discuss your dating problems over lattes or dim sum. We are big believers in talking with your BFFs so you don't act out with guys. You can ask a friend what to give a guy you just met for Valentine's Day (nothing!) so you don't end up writing hearts on his wall or buying him a mouse pad with your photo on it.

Women who are obsessed with guys really test the patience of their friends. They are so busy posting, "Happy 14-day anniversary!" on their new boyfriend's Facebook page that they hardly hear anything their friends say. No matter what the conversation is—midterms or the Middle East—these non-*Rules* Girls manage to bring up the guy. "I'm really sorry your mother's in the hospital. I hope she feels better soon. Did I tell you Jay's mom is a doctor? Jay is thinking about going to medical school. He just doesn't know if he wants to be an internist or a cardiologist." These women seem to have blinders on. They can't think about anything or anyone else, and this makes them downright rude or even obnoxious to their friends.

Elizabeth, a freshman, had a crush on Daniel, a junior who lived in her dorm. They were just friends, but then they hooked up twice after getting drunk at a frat party and Elizabeth became obsessed. She made her best friend, Madison, sit with her at the dining hall from the time it opened at 4:30 p.m. until it closed at 7 p.m. so she could run into Daniel. They sat there pretending to eat for three hours while Elizabeth weaved Daniel's name into every conversation.

"Did you say sushi? OMG, that's so funny, Daniel loves sushi. I'm hoping he takes me to his favorite sushi place over spring break."

"Are you going to the gym after dinner? I'll come with you. Daniel said he usually works out at around eight p.m. It would be so cool if we worked out together. He can see how hot I look on the treadmill. I'm going to my room to change into cute shorts…"

"How was your sister's wedding last week? I wish her better luck than Daniel's parents! He just told me they are getting divorced after thirty years. Can you imagine? Maybe I should text him and see how he's doing. He said it's really been hard on his younger sister. Maybe I should friend her on Facebook?"

Understandably, Madison was nauseated! Everything was Daniel this and Daniel that. And the few times when Daniel did walk into the cafeteria, Elizabeth actually left Madison alone at their table to sit next to him. Talk about rude!

He never called Elizabeth or asked her out, which of course resulted in her texting Madison to play guessing games as to what Daniel could be busy with. "He's probably studying like crazy. I read on his Facebook page that he's hitting the library every night. He wants to go to law school and I guess being in a relationship might be too much, I don't know. Or maybe stuff with his parents' divorce. Maybe I should call him. What do you think?" Madison had had it, but she was loyal and didn't want to hurt Elizabeth's feelings, so she said, "Yeah, that must be it" or "Sure, why don't you send him a quick text? Let him know you're thinking about him, but no pressure."

One evening, after yet another evening in the cafeteria,

Madison summoned the courage to tell Elizabeth, "If a guy skips two weeks, it's kind of over, don't you think? Why don't we go to an off-campus party and meet some new guys?" But Elizabeth's obsession had her over the edge. She went crazy on her good friend. "Can't you give a guy some slack? His parents are getting divorced and he has like three exams this week. Every guy isn't a robot with no feelings or issues. I think I'm going to write on his wall 'good luck with your physics midterm' and buy him special cupcakes. I just know it's the right thing to do."

When Daniel finally told Elizabeth that he couldn't handle a relationship right now, she still wouldn't accept it. "Why are you saying this? You're probably just stressed out, let's talk about it another time," she told him. It wasn't until he stopped answering her texts that she finally got the message. She felt devastated and alone. When she texted Madison and her other girlfriends to whine, they showed little sympathy. She even got one text back that said, "sorry, TTYL." She had burned her bridges with all of them and they had found better things to do than listen to her pity party. If you recognize yourself here *at all*, stop before it's too late, or you'll be all alone!

Elizabeth's story should be a cautionary tale to all women: don't ignore or dump your girlfriends just because you are obsessed with a guy. If the relationship ends or even never happens, you're going to need your BFFs to talk to and help you pick up the pieces of your heart from the floor!

Not only are girls like Elizabeth bad at maintaining friendships, but they can be a bad influence as well. Because they break *Rules* with guys, they might try to get you to do the same, if only because they don't know any better. They might suggest you friend a guy you like on Facebook or text him first or ask him out. They might say, "You're no fun" if you don't go along with their man-chasing ways. That's why we suggest finding other *Rules* Girls to talk to so you are less likely to deviate from your dating plan, and that's why we created a worldwide *Rules* contact system and *Rules* Facebook page—so you can find positive influences and support each other.

Don't be so obsessed with a guy that you become that kind of girlfriend. Don't be so obsessed with a guy that you forget your BFFs' birthdays or forget to wish them luck on their first day of work at a new job or to follow up if they have a medical scare. Whether it's a crush or a boyfriend, we can all get off track sometimes, but we must work extra hard to be good to our friends!

Don't Introduce a Guy to Anyone First, Invite Him Anywhere First, or Friend His Friends First

THESE DAYS, NO one is separated by more than six degrees. The world may have more people in it, but it's definitely getting smaller; everyone is a friend of a friend—of a friend. With all this connecting and reconnecting, you can suddenly be linked to nine hundred people and not even think twice about it!

But some women are using and abusing social networking sites to "meet" a guy's friends or family before he has made an official introduction. They feel that getting friendly with his people will bring them closer to him or help seal the deal. We understand the temptation to put his buddies, coworkers, mother, sister, or cousin on your radar, but it's a big mistake to make the first move into his world without his say-so. His friends and family might find it aggressive or even weird and creepy for you to invade their cyberspace—and it could backfire if they tell him that.

What's so bad about sending his mom a Facebook message to ask about her chicken soup recipe? Where's the harm in posting on his frat brother's wall how awesome their party was last weekend? Much like writing on *his* wall, in such situations you're pursuing his people, which is totally against

The Rules. It can be interpreted as borderline stalker-ish and might scare him away. It will make a guy, even one who initially pursued you, feel suffocated. You appear too involved in his business when you should barely notice who his friends are! It's like ringing his best friend's doorbell when you happen to be walking by instead of waiting for the guy you are dating to introduce you. It has pushy and eager written all over it! You want the guy you are dating to introduce you when he is ready, and accept their friend requests when they are ready to make them. That way he is more likely to preface his introduction with "This is the girl I've been telling you so much about," as opposed to "This is the girl who friended you and has been begging to meet you."

The key is that you have to do *The Rules* not only on him but also on his friends and family—he and anyone in his world must make the first move, online and off. You get to keep your own life, friends, and interests, and are able to avoid losing yourself in his. Don't message his seventeen-year-old sister on Facebook, "Text me if you want someone to go shopping with for a prom dress." She has her brother's ear and will tell him if she thinks it's weird! Instead, you should be hitting the mall with your own girlfriends on the weekend. Give time and attention to the important people in *your* world, not his!

This kind of aggressive behavior doesn't always involve friends and family, though. Some women always conveniently have extra hockey tickets and think nothing of wanting to ask the guy they are dating to join them for the game. Has he invited you anywhere like that yet? If he's taken you out only to drinks or to dinner, then the answer is no. Inviting a guy to a concert, sporting event, or family/work event is taking the relationship to the next level, not to mention asking him out.

An overture of this kind is not *The Rules*. Take a friend or coworker—anybody but him!

If you are going to a wedding, you might want to invite the guy you are seeing as your plus one. Has he ever invited you as his date to an event? If not, take anybody but him! The same goes for holiday dinners with your family, fundraisers, work functions, or formal events. Even if your social calendar is fuller than his—more of your friends are getting married or throwing parties or your job involves attending black-tie events—you can't invite him first to an event without being the pursuer. Above all else, it's asking him out! A guy will feel like you are planning your future together if you bring him into your world before he brings you into his, even if he seems initially flattered and excited to accompany you. He must set the tone for making introductions and bringing you into his work events, his Super Bowl shindigs, his parents' house, his world.

Kyle, twenty-nine, invited her thirty-two-year-old boyfriend of three months, Adam, to be her date for a black-tie business dinner. Kyle was dreading going alone and also wanted to show Adam off to her coworkers, who she had been gushing to about him in anticipation of their meeting. Adam seemed thrilled to join her when he agreed to go, but then two weeks before the event, he said work was really crazy for him and he wasn't sure he would be able to make it. Needless to say, she was annoyed and anxious. She called us in a tizzy, wanting to know how much she should push the issue because the calligrapher needed his name for the seating card. "Calligrapher"??? That's a *wedding* word—was she trying to scare him away? All a new guy has to see is his name etched next to hers on a seating card and he will think things are getting way too serious way too fast. We told her to invite a *friend*, male or female, to the event, and just have the calligrapher write "guest." Even if she did take Adam to any events in the future, he should still be listed as "guest." She asked if she should tell her boyfriend that he didn't have to go after all. We said not to bother—he probably forgot and would be relieved if she didn't mention it. Sure enough, she didn't bring it up and neither did he.

Carly invited a guy she had been dating for a month to her twenty-fifth-birthday party, thrown by her friends and family at her favorite restaurant. It was a casual event, but in a matter of hours, a guy who spoke to her first at a bar and had three Saturday night dates with her met her parents, her siblings, and closest friends from college and work. Carly called us a few weeks later to tell us that he'd told her he wasn't looking for anything serious. He hadn't asked her out in two weeks—since the party! After we did some digging, Carly added that one of her friends had asked the guy if he was her boyfriend and he had said, "We're just friends." She wanted to ask him what he meant by that considering she had slept with him on the last date—but we told her not to! Had he invited her to his birthday or to meet his friends or family? No, his birthday was six months away. Clearly, it had been a mistake to invite him to her party—he felt overwhelmed by meeting everyone she knew so quickly and all at once.

If your birthday comes before his, it's a tricky situation. If you are dating a guy for just a month or two and your birthday is coming up and your friends are talking about having a big bash, tell them you want to go low-key this year. The last thing you want is to be in the position of inviting him or not inviting him. If you do invite him, you run the risk of having him meet everyone in your life including your mother and thinking it's getting way too serious. If you don't include him, he might be insulted. Do yourself a favor and just celebrate your birthday with a few girlfriends over dinner.

An Invitation Loophole

What about huge birthday bashes and blowouts? Especially in college and into your early to mid-twenties, birthdays are a time to go big. More often than not, you might find yourself wanting to invite your entire Facebook friends list to celebrate your special day with you on the dance floor of your favorite club. Excluding the object of your affection from such an event might come off as a deliberate snub—even as a bit weird—and could possibly call more attention to your crush than you intended. So *should* you invite him? Sure—but be smart about it. Put one of your friends in charge of creating the Facebook event page and inviting everyone, or ask her to send out the mass e-mail to a guest list of your choosing. That way, he gets an invite, but you still haven't broken any *Rules*. And who knows? You might just end up getting the gift of a birthday dance with that special someone.

—Rules Daughters

Now, what if he asks if he can attend or asks if he is invited to an upcoming event? If it's a more formal event like a wedding or work function, say you're so sorry, you would like to, but you can't bring anyone—and go alone. Zoey, twenty-five, was invited to a wedding and hoped to bring Andy, her boyfriend of two months, as her date, but the bride said that she could not bring anyone because she had too many guests. Zoey asked us if she should beg her friend to make an exception, but we told her no. Not only would that have been impolite, but it also wasn't *The Rules*, since he had not invited her to anything comparable. So when Andy asked her to go out that Saturday night, she told him she couldn't see him because she had other plans. He asked what the plans were and she said, "My friend's wedding." Puzzled as to why Zoey didn't invite him but too well mannered to say anything, he simply asked her to meet for brunch and a movie the next day. Sunday at 11 a.m., Andy showed up at her apartment, demanding to know who she took and who she danced with. Zoey told him the truth, as *Rules* Girls don't lie, that she had had only one invitation to the wedding and she danced with her girlfriends. Andy was relieved to hear the good news, but had clearly been shaken, wondering all night who her plus one was. This curiosity made Andy like Zoey even more! *The Rules* worked—they are married now.

If you are thinking about initiating the move into each other's worlds, think again. Let him take the lead with this concept, as with everything else. Let him suggest your meeting his friends and his meeting your friends—and act nonchalant about it when he does. The problem today is that women are introducing men to everyone and inviting them to everything. Big mistake! Think long term. Do you want a date for a wedding or a permanent plus one?

Don't Write to Guys First, Ignore Winks, and Other *Rules* for Online Dating

SOME SINGLE WOMEN have a problem with online dating. Either they think it's not for them and refuse to do it, or they do it the wrong way. We feel that there are only two mistakes you can make with online dating. The first is not to try it. (We will get to the second in a minute.) If you are afraid or embarrassed to try online dating, we are here to tell you that it's a safe and viable way to meet guys. When women complain to us that they can't meet anyone, we suggest that, in addition to speed-dating and other singles events, they join a dating website. You would think we were telling them to pose for *Playboy*! They feel that it's too public—what will their boss or neighbor say?—or insist that they have tried it before and it doesn't work.

Here are some of the reactions we get to the idea of online dating—and our responses:

- **"I'm too shy."** There is no social interaction involved in signing up! You just put together a profile with some photos, and let guys do the work!

- **"I would die if people I know saw it."** Hello, that means they're on the site, too! Nothing to be ashamed of.

- **"I tried it and didn't meet anyone good."** You probably didn't give it enough time. Also, your profile is not exactly *Rules*-y!

- **"Only losers go online."** Our clients who met their husbands online would beg to differ! The guys on these dating sites are a microcosm of *all* single guys: some are cute and normal, others are not. What else is new?

- **"Most online guys are married!"** Sure, some are, but most aren't. *The Rules* screen out married guys anyway because they don't ask you out consistently on Saturday nights or on holidays!

- **"I don't have a good or recent photo."** That's easy to fix—just ask a friend to take one, or you can even use a professional photographer!

No matter how many other ways you are trying to date, getting online will only increase your chances of meeting a great guy. It's a legitimate social outlet—thousands of women have met their husbands online, probably including someone you know—and it's not dangerous if done the right way. Trying to meet someone at bars and singles events is time-consuming and not always possible if you have a job with busy hours or young children. Furthermore, the kind of guy you want may not be hanging out there anyway. Online dating is easy *and* convenient.

Perhaps the most compelling reason to try it is that as you get older, the dating pool gets smaller. More of your friends become engaged or married and have no one to introduce you to or aren't eager to play your wing woman. After college, you won't necessarily meet guys easily or by accident like you did on campus. Getting online is just another way to meet people—there's nothing weird or scary about it! Sure, you might meet some frogs before you meet your prince, but that will happen offline, too!

Once you get past your resistance to online dating, it's time to focus on putting together your profile. The first step is to create your user name. Many women are tempted to use something generic that makes them difficult to identify, like their initials and birth date, but that is a mistake. Inventing what is essentially a nickname for yourself on a dating website is an opportunity for creativity in making the right impression. Why not take advantage of it? We like to figure out what popular actress or model a girl resembles because celebrity look-alikes always catch attention. Another option is to capitalize on your favorite traits. "BlakeLivelyGal" and "BlueEyedLawyer32" are good examples of user names. Sometimes clients ask, "But isn't it conceited to say I look like a movie star?" No—it's fun and shows great self-esteem! More importantly, it will catch a guy's attention. Besides, who wouldn't want to feel like he is dating a celebrity? Emma, thirty-three, wrote that she was a Kim Kardashian look-alike and got a message that said, "I hope *our* marriage lasts longer than three months!"

Since men are attracted to a certain look/type, the photo you choose to put on your profile is extremely important—just as your appearance would be offline. We see too many photos in which the woman is posing with her niece or wearing a tawdry Halloween costume; she is squinting or her hair is a mess; her boobs are popping out of her bikini top or the arm of a man who has been cropped out hangs over her shoulder. Have someone take new photos specifically for use on your dating profile. Smile and face the camera—no brooding or overly artistic pictures. Ideally, you'll have one head shot and one or two body shots so that you can show men the whole package.

In terms of the actual content of the profile, we think it's best to keep it short and sweet. Focus on surface items, like your profession, hobbies, and favorite shows, movies, foods, sports, and travel spots. Here is one example of a *Rules*-y profile:

PrettyPublicist32

Blake Lively Look-alike

I went to Georgetown U. and work as a beauty product publicist in NYC. When I am not working, I like to go running, biking, swimming, and to the movies. My favorite movie is *Titanic* and my favorite TV show is *Law & Order.* I like sushi and Italian food. I like going out to LA once a year. Looking for someone smart and athletic, with a good sense of humor.

Sometimes clients will say that their *Rules*-y self-description is too short or too shallow, preferring to tell guys more about their passions and inner selves. They want their unique personalities to shine through many paragraphs about their thoughts, feelings, and opinions, their past and future; they want to share their experience, strength, and hope about life, love, and relationships. For example, some women write, "I don't play games and I'm looking for someone to bond with—someone who completes me, but is not codependent." Others will write that they are looking for someone "who is not threatened by a strong, financially independent woman," or be up front that they are "not *bitter* for having gone through a bad divorce, but *better*!" They want to write a résumé or spill all their thoughts as if their profile were an autobiography, fearing that five sentences about their favorite things will not do them justice. But as usual, less is more! Even if you're filling in separate fields in your profile, guys basically look at photos and only skim the rest. We have found that women who write dissertations attract pen pals who want to delve even deeper online, but don't ask them out.

Women who share less, especially those with good screen names and photos, attract guys who are intrigued and ask them out. The trick is just to pique their interest. So if you have done online dating before and had no luck, we suggest you try it again with pretty photos and just a few facts—see if you get better results!

The second mistake we referred to at the beginning of this chapter is initiating contact with a guy through the site. The cardinal *Rule* for online dating is that he writes to you first. You never message or send him a wink or chat him up first, no matter how perfect or your type he is. To do so is just like talking to him first in person. It is pursuing his look/ type, personality, photos, and interests, which makes you the aggressor—it's against the entire concept of *The Rules*. We have found that most of the time online relationships in which the woman wrote first did not work out. The only time it has worked is when a guy was actually about to contact her but she beat him to the punch—she was very lucky. As with everything else, it's best to wait for the guy to make the first move so you don't have any doubts about how interested he really is.

You should also ignore winks, flirts, and other similar actions on dating websites. These are when a guy clicks on your profile but doesn't write to you. It's the equivalent of looking at you at a party but not approaching you or speaking to you—in other words, a big nothing. We tell women to ignore winks because there's no effort involved. It's like poking you on Facebook instead of writing a message. If a man can't even send an e-mail to introduce himself, then he probably won't ask you out either.

How to answer a guy's message to your online profile is an art form for a *Rules* Girl. We keep it brief because we are not looking for a pen-pal relationship, but rather for dates. We want to go from online to offline as quickly as possible— within four exchanges, to be exact. If a guy does not ask you out within four messages, he is either a time waster, not that interested in you, or in a relationship. Next! As with every medium of communication, you should wait at least four hours to write back to a new guy who answered your online profile, but if you are thirty and older, you can wait a whole day to write back. (You can refer to our Text-Back Times chart on page 66.)

If a guy writes, "You are very pretty. We have a lot in common. Have you been on this site long? How do you like it? Look at my profile and let me know what you think," do not discuss his profile with him and bond over all your common interests. Of course you can read it, but do not tell him you did—that shows too much interest. Instead, write a generic "Thanks. You seem interesting!" That will force him to say something like "I noticed you like Italian food. Any favorite places?" Then you can write back, "I like such-and-such place." Then he can cut to the chase and write back, "Would you like to meet there one night this week?" If you go on and on about your interests and his interests and how long you have been online and what your experiences have been, you will be chatting online forever. If he has so many questions, he can take you out for drinks!

Remember, you never want to seem like you live for online dating! You are busy and have other things going on in your life. Hence, in addition to a response wait time, the weekend is a dead zone here, too. If a guy reaches out to you on Friday at 7 p.m., don't answer four hours later; wait until Sunday night.

Here are some other important *Rules*:

- **Safety comes first.** Online guys are strangers, so never use your full name or the name of your company in your screen name. You are BlondeBanker, not ChelseaJones @gmail.com or CJones@NatwestBank.com. Do not specify where you live or work. You can say you're a realtor, but avoid saying you work at MiamiRiches Realtors in Florida. On the first date, meet somewhere public, like at a Starbucks or for drinks at a restaurant near you. Tell a friend where you are and to call or text you after an hour, just in case. Do not get into his car or let him get into yours, no matter how insane the chemistry is— and do not sleep with the guy right away. If you didn't meet at work or through friends, then you don't really know him, so be careful!

- **Turn off the instant-messaging feature** on the online dating website, if it has one, so you are not so accessible and he cannot see when you are using the site. Stay mysterious!

- **If a guy you met online continues to contact you and ask you out via e-mail, even after the first date, do not suggest "bringing it to the phone."** A date is a date. If he's not into the phone, you have to live with it or stop seeing him. Besides, you knew from the beginning that he was into the latest technology.

- **If a guy sends you his number, but doesn't ask for yours, you can reciprocate by responding, "OK, great, and my number is _____."** The only way to know if a guy is in the mood to talk to you is when *he* calls you.

- **Screen out buyer-beware guys.** If he doesn't post a photo, ask to see one when you respond to his message. Do not agree to meet a guy who hasn't sent you a photo. You're not being superficial—he's just being suspicious. Also skip guys who talk about sex in their profiles or messages. Be wary of guys who send vague or form letters that make no mention of anything specific in your profile.

- **Don't have a "Romeo and Juliet" relationship with online guys you have never met.** If a guy has not asked you out within four e-mails, it's a fantasy cyberspace relationship, so move on. How can a woman fall in love and even break up with a guy without ever meeting him? Some women talk to bored or lonely men whom they never meet, but whom they swear they have a soul connection with. To have a connection, you have to meet. Dating is rarely like *Sleepless in Seattle*!

- **Don't take your profile down until you are in an exclusive relationship and he has removed his as well.** If he tells you that he "just has not gotten around to it yet," don't believe him! Invariably, this type is still looking at other women's profiles, despite professing monogamy with you. So keep dating!

- **Last but not least, don't take yourself off an online dating site until you find who you're looking for.** Women decide to "take a break" from online dating or decide not to renew when their six-month subscription runs out. That's crazy! What is there to take a break from— meeting your future boyfriend? Would you take a break from checking online job boards if you hadn't found a job? We didn't think so! Sure, you can take a break by not answering your e-mails for a few days here and there, but if you really want to meet a guy, keep your profile up for as long as necessary, in addition to going out once or twice a week. You have to be in it to win it—don't drop out of the game!

Rule #19 _____

Don't Pay for Dinner or Buy His Love in Any Way

WOMEN WHO DO too much or give too much in relationships are the subject of entire self-help books. We will save you the trouble of reading them by telling you that if you have to do more than agree to go on dates for a guy to like you, then you are doing too much!

It is desperate and not *The Rules* to meet him halfway for a date, pay for dinner, take him on vacation, or buy his love in any way. Buying him gifts and splitting the cost of trips are both "nice" ways women try to ingratiate themselves with men, but it just won't make a guy love them! Women who overdo it are spoiling guys, but we know that guys really desire women who don't try hard at all. Worse, though, it's manipulative—you are trying to make it easy for him to be with you. A *Rules* Girl doesn't have to give a guy a reason to be with her by "roping him in" with her frequent-flier miles or credit card. She *is* the reason!

When you give too much in the beginning of a relationship, a guy will sense it and lose interest. It is another way in which you become the pursuer and it becomes obvious that you like him. In addition, guys have pride and don't want to be supported, even if they initially go along with a woman's generosity. Brenda, a thirty-five-year-old CEO, was dating her yoga instructor. She let him stay at her city apartment on nights that he worked late, hoping that would lead to exclusivity. After some time passed, she suggested he move in so he wouldn't have to commute to the suburbs (and really so that they could be together more often). A few weeks after they started living together, Brenda found text messages to other women on his phone. When she confronted him, he claimed, "I never said we were exclusive. It was your idea that I live here, not mine." He wasn't even grateful for his rent-free accommodations! Brenda called us hysterically crying because she had thought he could be The One. We told her to have him pack his bags right away. More importantly, we told her not to try to lure or trap a guy with her money, possessions, or perks, especially not to keep a relationship going. It never works!

It's no secret that some women today are out-earning the men they are dating. Some of these women think nothing of using their money and influence to keep a guy interested. We have clients in high-powered positions or ones in family businesses who try to get guys they just met jobs at their company or their father's firm. Not a good idea! If you get him an interview or a job, you will never know if he is dating you because of your connections or because he really likes *you*. The only way to know is to give him *nothing*.

Nothing means not paying for things or doing him favors like getting him the perks of your job, whatever those are. If a guy you are dating says he doesn't have the money to take you out for nice dinners, say, "That's okay!" He can take you somewhere inexpensive or come up with another creative idea. Do not respond by offering to pay. If he asks to borrow money so he can do nice things for you, just tell him you don't have it.

Randi, a twenty-nine-year-old optometrist, was dating a

struggling novelist named Michael. She paid for their dinners and also lent him money to pay his rent. Michael broke up with her after a year of dating when he coincidentally landed a six-figure book deal, claiming he was not ready for a serious relationship. What?! She was out almost $5,000! Randi wanted to e-mail him about getting her money back, but we told her to forget it and move on—she could sell the necklace he gave her. We've even heard of women who lent money to guys and sued them for it after the relationship ended. It can be messy and unpleasant to say the least. Just don't do it!

Maybe he has been spoiled by other women who split everything, but that's not your problem! Or he might say that his ex-girlfriend was a gold digger and he doesn't want to be used again and that's why he's so cautious about money. To that, just respond with your apologies, but still avoid paying for anything of great value. Guys are ingenious when they are looking for a free ride—don't fall for it! You don't have to break up with him if everything else is good, but you need to silently show him that you are not going to be his sugar mama. It's not about the money, it's about the fact that a guy has to pursue or he won't appreciate you! If you start paying, you may feel the tables turning in the relationship.

Women have many ways of being generous. They buy him a watch or an iPad. They walk through his apartment and decide he needs a bigger TV. They turn into his free interior decorator and leave their imprints all over his place, so he remembers *their* wineglasses and napkin holders. Or they rummage through his closet and decide he needs a new suit or a good leather jacket. They buy him an expensive tie or monogrammed cufflinks for his annual review with his boss. If they have an upcoming business trip or extra frequent-flier miles, they pay for him to tag along. If they work in an industry with lots of perks, they invite him to cocktail parties and fancy dinners and send a car service to pick him up. Of course he loves all her presents and perks, but that doesn't mean he loves her! Take our advice and save your money and wife-y generosity for when you are married. After you are married, you can decorate your love nest, buy him presents, make him your plus one on business trips and at parties—but not when you're dating.

Gifts for Him

We had to consult our moms a little bit for this one. We agree it's important not to buy a boyfriend's love, but can't we get him something nice on his birthday? Birthdays are one of the only days a year when giving is not just encouraged, it's expected—and no one wants to be known as the girlfriend who didn't get her guy something nice. Picking the perfect present can be really stressful! Obvious things to avoid include anything extravagant (like a new iPod or an expensive watch) as well as anything mega-mushy (leave your scrapbooking supplies locked up!). At the end of the day, it's always best to get him something thoughtful that doesn't break the bank: a T-shirt of his favorite sports team, a DVD of a movie he loves, a special dinner out, or even a romantic home-cooked meal! You don't have to spend a lot to show you care.

—*Rules Daughters*

If you have been dating exclusively for a long time, you can pay for little things here and there. For example, if your boyfriend is taking you to dinner and a show, you can buy him drinks or take him somewhere nice for dessert. If he is sick, you can bring him chicken soup in bed and bring him a variety of cold medicines. But for regular Saturday night dinner dates, he should be picking up the tab.

If a guy insists that you go away with him but expects you to split the cost of the trip, say, "Thanks, but I don't think I can take the time off" and skip it. Buyer beware: he may not be in love with you and may just be looking for a travel companion to have fun with. What if you have been dating for a while and he invites you to go away and is really excited about it? Sometimes dating and traveling require firm negotiation! Once he agrees to a time frame that is good for you—no longer than four days—let him plan the trip, make all the arrangements, and put it on *his* credit card. If he asks you to pay for something or you feel it's right to contribute, pick one thing, like your airfare, and pay for that only. For example, if he asks you to go on a four-day cruise, you can pay for the off-boat excursions. Never put the whole trip (airfare, hotel, restaurants) on your credit card with the idea that he will reimburse you, as sometimes it will be awkward or impossible to get your money back. Sometimes a guy will have sudden business problems or bills right after a trip and you will feel heartless asking for your money, especially if you make more than he does or he has student loans and you don't. (Money aside, the other reason not to go away for a week or two is that familiarity breeds contempt. Save *that* trip for your honeymoon.)

Money and material items are not the only ways women try to woo a guy and worm their way into his life. They e-mail him poetry, make collages of all the places they've been to, and become groupies at his sporting events. They try to patch up the fight he had with his father. They play therapist when he has a bad day or when he wants to talk about his ex-girlfriend. Do you recognize yourself here?

If you are a generous person, then help your friends or find a charity and do volunteer work. But don't use your positive qualities as an excuse to do or buy things for a guy you are dating, because you will be putting yourself in a position to be used or hurt. Whether you're giving him money for a car tune-up, cleaning his apartment for him, or getting him an interview at your law firm—it's too much. You should not have to work that hard to get a guy's interest. A *Rules* Girl doesn't have to buy a guy's love or attention. If you are doing more than going on dates and being a CUAO, then you are doing too much!

Don't Choose a College or Job or Relocate Because of a Guy

THERE ARE MANY factors that go into picking the right college, career, or city for yourself. Deciding where you'll go to school or work or live solely based on your boyfriend or crush can be a big and costly mistake. Women of all ages can succumb to this temptation.

Isabella, a thirty-five-year-old lawyer, met Mark, thirty-eight, a senior lawyer at the same firm, when he flew in from San Francisco to the company's headquarters in Chicago to work on a special case. Mark, who had a reputation for getting whatever he wanted, was smitten from the moment he met the tall brunette beauty. He made it his business to travel to Chicago twice a month for four-day weekends just to see her. They had a whirlwind courtship: daily textfests, e-mails, Skype sessions, fancy dinners, and jewelry! After six months, Mark asked Isabella to move to San Francisco so he could get to know her even better and hinted about a ring and a proposal. Isabella fell for her legal knight in shining armor.

Without much thought, she sold her condo, left her family and friends, accepted a transfer to the San Francisco office for a job with less seniority, and moved in with Mark. Because of all the concessions she had made, she figured Mark would propose within a month or two. But after six months of living together and no ring or proposal, Isabella started feeling depressed and angry. She had few friends and no wedding to plan. Mark started working late because he was up for partner. Every time she brought up getting engaged, Mark became irritated and said, "What's the rush? Let's take our time. Besides, you don't seem much like the girl I met any-more." The argument would incense Isabella even more. She told him, "I'm this way because you still haven't proposed." It became a chicken-and-egg situation between them. It kept going back and forth.

When Isabella contacted us crying, we were not surprised to hear that things had soured. We explained that when you relocate to a guy's city without a formal commitment (a ring and a wedding date), the guy gets complacent about mar-riage (surely your grandmother has said, "Why buy the cow when you have the milk for free?"), while you get ballistic that you uprooted your life for nothing. We told Isabella to tell Mark that she could no longer live with him without a ring and a wedding date and to start packing her bags if he didn't propose. He got angry and said he refused to have a gun put to his head. Isabella moved out as quickly as pos-sible and returned to Chicago—and never heard from Mark again. She lost a year of her life to a guy who didn't want to marry her. So no matter how exciting relocating seems, don't be impulsive.

Of course, Isabella is not the first working woman to waste time by relocating to be with her boyfriend. But it's mostly college girls who don't think twice about changing schools or moving to be with their boyfriends without any commitment. Aside from compromising your education or future career, transferring to a college to be closer to your boyfriend makes you the pursuer and sometimes even a stalker. Most college guys want to have their freedom. They are not ready to settle down; they want to experiment and have fun, not be glued to your hip. If you follow a guy to college, he might get claustrophobic and dump you.

We have spoken to young women who made the dreadful decision to follow their boyfriends or crushes to college and lived to regret it. They gave up their academic dreams and self-esteem to schlep hundreds of miles away, only to have the guys break up with them during spring break or finals. There is nothing more awkward and embarrassing than bumping into your college boyfriend on campus with his new squeeze!

Ashley and Dylan had been together since their junior year of high school. Dylan had spoken to her first and asked if she wanted to study together. When it came time to pick colleges, Ashley wanted to stay local, but Dylan set his sights on a college two thousand miles away that specialized in sports medicine, despite her interest in nutrition. Ashley talked her parents into letting her apply to Dylan's school, but Dylan's response was hardly enthusiastic: "Are you sure you want to do this? Aren't you going to miss your parents? You're so close." That was guy code for "Don't follow me, I'm young and I still want to date other girls." But Ashley thought he was just being polite and decided to ignore this red flag. She was so afraid that she would lose Dylan to another girl if their relationship became long distance that she was determined to make it work: "Don't worry, I'll text them every day," she told him.

At college, Ashley never let Dylan out of her sight. She was always hanging out in his room, trying to figure out ways to get rid of his roommate. She tracked Dylan down at the cafeteria for breakfast, lunch, and dinner. For Dylan's birthday, she gave him a Hallmark card and a $100 gift certificate to a sporting goods store. For her birthday a month later, Dylan scrawled "Happy Birthday" with a Sharpie on the back of his math homework and promised to give her "something special soon."

Three months later, Ashley invited Dylan to Thanksgiving dinner at her parents' house, but he told her he was buying a bus ticket to visit a friend at a nearby college. Ashley felt rejected and told him maybe they should break up, hoping he would talk her out of it. Instead he said, "I think so, too." Shocked, Ashley started studying Dylan's Facebook page for clues and figured out that his "friend" was his ex-girlfriend and that they were back together. Ashley flew home for Thanksgiving sobbing. Her parents convinced her to transfer to a local college to study nutrition—as originally planned.

Nothing good ever comes from following a guy to college. In fact, we have spoken to guys and they all said, "Don't do it!" One guy said he had to break up with a girl just to keep her from transferring to be with him. He was only twenty-one and not looking to settle down—he didn't want her to change her life for him. If you don't want to suffer pain and humiliation and come across as a stalker, don't follow a guy anywhere! The only way it works is if the guy follows you! Let him pursue you through the medium of location, as well as every other way we've discussed in this book.

Here is another true story, but with a different ending:

Emily and her boyfriend, Jake, were high school sweethearts for three years. He was a year older and opted to go to a college nearby. Emily wanted to do the same, but her parents wouldn't hear of it. They wanted her to go away to get some life experience and expand her social life.

Emily was so upset after saying good-bye to Jake in August that she didn't even speak to her parents on the four-hour car drive to freshman move-in day. As it turned out, her parents were right. She had a wonderful roommate, joined a sorority, made new friends, and loved being away. Jake missed her so much that he posted on her Facebook wall and sent her e-mails every day. He also suggested Skype sessions every night at 9 p.m. to make sure she was in her room and not out with other guys! He visited her every other week and was with her every holiday. Eventually, he got so sick and tired of commuting and being apart that *he* transferred to *her* school. Shortly after college graduation, he proposed. They are now happily married.

In Emily's case, her parents did *The Rules* for her by not letting her follow Jake to college. If they hadn't, would Jake have fought so hard to be with her? Would he have felt suffocated or confused if she followed him to his school? Would they be married today if Emily had made it so easy for him? Maybe not!

If you are thinking about following your boyfriend to college or relocating to be with him for any reason, don't do it. You can screw up your academic life or career and waste a lot of time, money, and energy, and lose the guy anyway. Until you are married or about to get married, you are the most important person in your life, and *your* dreams and goals should be the factors in choosing your location.

Don't Get Wasted on Dates or at Parties, So You Don't Say or Do Anything You'll Regret

WE HATE TO say it, but we know that drinking is a rite of passage. At many colleges, especially those with frat houses and football teams, pre-game and tailgating parties are all the rage. Drinking is also a great social lubricant after college at networking and professional events. Alcohol takes away inhibitions and gets a conversation going. We get it. We think it's great if you can have a drink or two and act *Rules*-y. But if you can't drink without embarrassing yourself and/or starting a fight with a guy, then drinking may not be for you.

Heavy drinking and dating do not mix. When you are under the influence of alcohol, you end up making bad decisions you wouldn't make otherwise, like saying yes to booty calls, ex-boyfriends, and even married men. You might sleep with a guy you just met because the part of your brain that says "This is not a good idea" doesn't work when you have had too much to drink. We have spoken to dozens of women who have said that alcohol has ruined their dating lives, both in and out of college. Obviously, it is almost impossible to do *The Rules* when your boundaries become blurry or non-existent. Instead of keeping the date light and breezy, you are spilling your guts because you are intoxicated. Instead of talking about school or work or movies on the first date, you are leaning over to kiss a guy and telling him you really like him. When you are drinking too much, you definitely forget to look at your watch and nonchalantly end the date first after two hours. After too many glasses of wine on your first or second date, you may have told him your whole life story, including why your ex-boyfriend dumped you. There's nothing worse than the feeling when you sober up hours later and can't believe what you said—or did! Girls who get embarrassingly drunk don't usually hear from guys again, except for 2 a.m. booty calls, even if it was their first time acting that way. A guy will assume that what you do with him, you do with everyone else. Having a reputation of being drunk and hooking up is not good. We polled guys in and out of college and they all said that girls who get drunk are a big turnoff.

We think one drink on a date is enough. We have heard from clients who had just two drinks at a dinner "to calm their nerves" and ended up saying or doing things they regret. Like it or not, alcohol changes the way you act. Alana, who is in her thirties, told us that every time she has more than one glass of wine, she ends up picking fights with her boyfriend of nine months, accusing him of having feelings for his secretary. She says things like "Are you sure you're not working late to be with her?" She once even hit him, despite the fact that he has said "I love you" and talks about the future. But when Alana is sober, she is sweet and this side of her doesn't come out. Alcohol can be like truth serum, making you say things that are better left in a diary or a *Rules* consultation! If drinking makes you go from being shy to dancing on tables or starting silly, jealous fights with a guy, you probably can't drink on dates.

Gabby, twenty-nine, told us that her four years in college

Be Cautious about Date Rape

Keeping track of your drinks might save you some
embarrassment on dates, but it can also help keep you safe
during a night out. On campus, you hear about date rape all
too often—stories of girls who drank too much and suffered
serious consequences. If you do decide to drink, be smart
about it. If a date-rape drug is slipped into your vodka soda,
all it takes is one, and sometimes guys don't even need a drug
to take advantage. A *Rules* Girl always needs to be prepared.
Don't ever put yourself in an isolated situation with a guy
you just met. Keep count of how many drinks you've had that
night. Avoid drinking punch at a party; you may know all
the guys there, but you *don't* know how much alcohol is really
in it, or if someone thought it would be fun to "spice up the
party." Always watch your drink being poured, or be sure
to open cans and bottles yourself. And if you're out partying
with friends, ask some of your girls to watch your back—the
buddy system isn't just for little kids! If some shady guy tries
to take advantage, he'll have your posse to deal with, and
then *he'll* be the one suffering the consequences.

—*Rules Daughters*

were a dating disaster because of her out-of-control drugging.
She said she snorted anything she could get because it took
away her inhibitions and gave her a real buzz. She would get
horribly wasted, throw up, pass out, or end up in a guy's bed.
Many mornings she couldn't remember what had happened,
or she would remember and be appalled at her behavior.
With each new guy she met, Gabby thought, "This time will
be different," but it never was. Her drugging and hooking

up went on through her early twenties because being young made her think she was invincible. But a few more blackouts, humiliating hookups, and a bad car crash after college were a serious reality check. While she was getting sober, Gabby found *The Rules*, did them, and met the man who became her husband. She knows now that drugs definitely impaired her decision-making with guys. Gabby was happy to share her story with us, hoping that other women might learn from her foolishness.

Drinking and drugging are usually used to numb painful feelings, fears, and low self-esteem ("I'm not pretty enough" or "I'll never have a boyfriend."). So if you want to "take the edge off" but can't control your consumption, you are better off texting your friends or your therapist and telling them how you feel. We understand that you want to let loose and have fun, but there is nothing fun about blacking out and hooking up. If you can't drink like a lady, then order a tonic or sparkling water. If you can't drink and do *The Rules*, then don't drink at all!

Buyer Beware...Weeding Out Bad Guys (Cheaters, Addicts, Players, and Time Wasters)

CAVEAT EMPTOR IS a Latin expression that means "buyer beware." But it doesn't apply only to decisions about merchandise—it also applies to men. What you see is what you get. *The Rules* are not just about getting a guy—but someone with good character you can trust, who will hopefully make a good boyfriend or future husband. Conversely, we call guys with questionable or unacceptable character or behavior "buyer bewares" and tell women to be careful or run the other way.

Simply put, *Rules* Girls do not put up with bad behavior. Love may be blind, but *Rules* Girls are not deaf or dumb. When you are dating a guy, you need to look for red flags right away so you don't find out six months or five years later that he is not for you. One of the reasons we tell women to talk and text less is so that they listen and read more and notice what may be good or bad about a guy. In this digital age, women can find out faster whether he is a good guy or a cheater, addict, player, or time waster.

A buyer-beware guy will not respond well to *The Rules*. He will not call or text in advance for plans, he will skip weeks or even your birthday, he will insist on splitting the bill, he will cancel, he will flirt with other girls, he will get wasted, he will play mind games, and he will make your life miserable.

Women ask us all the time, "How do I know if my boyfriend is cheating?" If you have to ask, you probably need to do a little detective work. Something just doesn't feel right. Maybe he gets a lot of texts when you're together, but doesn't say anything about them. Maybe he has a password on his phone or he never lets it out of his sight, which is odd behavior if you are comfortable and in an intimate relationship. When a text message comes through on his phone, he acts strangely secretive.

Naturally our clients want to know if it's okay to check his texts, private Facebook messages, and e-mails. That's a personal decision, but it might be better to get a definitive answer now than to wonder or find out later on. Of course, by the time a woman is checking or even considering checking her boyfriend's laptop or phone, she already senses something is wrong. Sometimes she gets lucky and the evidence just falls into her lap and she doesn't have to snoop. He might leave his phone on his desk when he takes a shower or goes for a run. Or he forgets to log off his Facebook account on her laptop. If she does find incriminating texts or e-mails to another woman, we discuss whether it is better to confront him or to track his behavior for a while so there is no doubt in her mind that he has been unfaithful. We generally think it's better not to confront a guy right away, for two reasons: you want to calm down and you want to have more evidence.

Keep in mind, though, that a cheater is usually a liar, too. When a client finally confronts her boyfriend with the trail of texts, he will usually deny that the other woman exists or say, "She's just a friend" or "That's my trainer." Often a guy will turn it around on his girlfriend and say, "You're crazy" or "You're being paranoid" or, worse, "Your reading them is just as bad as my sending them." Snooping is nothing to be proud of, we agree. But cheating is a lot worse. When he starts blaming *you* for his cheating, then you really know he is a buyer beware and the relationship is over!

In these situations, it's almost always best to end the relationship and not look back, as cheating is a deal breaker and is never to be taken lightly. But some women are so in love or heartbroken that they can't fathom ending the relationship and want to give the guy a second chance. They become obsessed with getting him back at any cost. They even ask the guy what was missing in the relationship and try to be "more fun" or "take up golf" or whatever he said it was, but it usually never works out. Once a cheater, always a cheater. Even if the boyfriend stops seeing the other woman and comes back to you, you'll be forever checking his phone to see what he's up to. It will be hell.

However, strong suspicions do not always a cheater make. We have had clients whose father cheated on their mother or whose ex-boyfriend cheated on them and they are convinced that every guy is unfaithful. We help them see via childhood and dating history consultations that their suspicions are not always the reality; sometimes it's all in their heads. Casey, who had an affair with a married man before her own marriage, often wondered if her husband was flirting with the women he meets at business lunches. But she has found no evidence in four years, and we have concluded that her suspicions have more to do with her own karma than with his behavior. Similarly, if your boyfriend cheated on his ex-girlfriend or ex-wife, you may fear that he will cheat on you—but that is not necessarily true. They probably did not have a *Rules* relationship, but you do. Even if your guy cheated on an ex, he will most likely be faithful to you if you did *The Rules*.

Sometimes a woman will complain that her boyfriend is a buyer beware when the problem is that she is doing *The Rules* too strictly. For example, she will be rude instead of busy, or impossible to get instead of just hard to get. Cindy was dating a notorious player and thought turning him down for a Saturday night date once a month would make him even more smitten. The only time to turn a guy down for a date is if he is behaving badly, like canceling plans or missing a special occasion (or, of course, if you really are busy). Her move didn't make him more smitten. It made him confused—so confused that he got drunk and texted his ex-girlfriend. Cindy sensed something was wrong on their next date; she checked his phone and saw the text exchanges. She confronted him and he explained that when she said she was busy, he was sure she was seeing someone else. It was a big misunderstanding and they are now engaged. Overdoing *The Rules* can definitely backfire if not executed properly. *The Rules* are strict enough!

Speaking of players, players are not necessarily buyer bewares—sometimes they are just guys who have never met a *Rules* Girl before! They have been spoiled by women who call and text them or see them last minute or sleep with them too soon. When they meet a *Rules* Girl, they are often pleasantly surprised because they respect a woman who has boundaries and self-esteem and they love a good challenge. A notorious player can definitely be caught by a *Rules* Girl! But some player types will respond well for a month or two and then get angry that you are not seeing them at a moment's notice or going away with them on weeklong trips. They blame you for not being more available. Some will even dump you and then suggest being "friends." They are either incorrigible or just not ready to commit. Next!

Other buyer-beware guys?

- **Guys who break up with you for any reason.** If he breaks up with you once, he can break up with you again. Guys who walk out on you or scream, "It's over!" are bound to hurt you again. You should think, "Good riddance" instead of "How can I get him back?" Your boyfriend should never want to stop being with you.

- **Guys who just want to be friends.** A guy who suggests being friends after you have slept together, met each other's friends and families, and shared special moments is a big buyer beware. He is *demoting* you, so do not be flattered that he wants to stay friends on Facebook and keep texting you. Don't meet for lunch, don't answer his texts, and definitely block him on Facebook and every other form of social media. He will just waste your time—precious time that you should be spending meeting new guys who ask you out! If you run into an ex who just wants to be friends at school or work or in your social circle, don't speak to him first, be polite if he speaks to you, and keep walking.

- **Guys who cancel more than once.** You can waste years with a guy who is always rescheduling! Refer to *Rule #24* for the details on this type of guy.

- **Guys who don't follow through.** Jill, a graduate student, was approached by a guy at a club who got her number and then texted her about going out on Saturday night. So far, so good. Then she didn't hear from him for the rest of the week. She texted him at 8 p.m. on Saturday night, "What happened? I thought we had a date!" He wrote back, "I forgot. Why didn't you text me sooner?" She wrote back, "I can't date a guy who forgets and doesn't follow thru!" He wrote back, "I can't date a girl who doesn't text me to remind me." Yikes! But she shouldn't have texted him in the first place—once he forgets, you forget. If you have to remind him that you have a date, then it's not a date you should be going on. And if he asks you out and then doesn't show up, it's over!

- **Guys who are extra work from day one.** Haley was introduced to a guy by a mutual friend who showed him her photo. She was in the middle of a business meeting the first time Joey texted her. He wrote her asking if he could call her in ten minutes—the first red flag, as he assumed she could drop everything in ten minutes to talk to him at work. Haley asked us what to do and we instructed her to text him back the next day, "Sorry I was busy in meetings all day." He texted back, "I thought I would hear from you sooner. Okay, call me when you're free." Haley wrote back an hour later, "Okay, or you can call me..." It was like a standoff, waiting to see who would pick up the phone first. He finally called her that night and set up their first date for drinks. But of course, it wasn't that simple. First he texted her to meet him near his office downtown. She wrote back, "It's better for me if we meet uptown around here." He then texted asking whether they could meet halfway, but as *Rules* Girls don't meet halfway, she texted back that she was too busy with work and he finally texted okay to that. We told Haley, brace yourself, this guy is going to be a handful—buyer beware! Their encounters felt like peace talks. Sure enough, he spent the one-hour drink date talking nonstop about his ex-girlfriend. We told her, Next! Run as fast as you can! He never called or texted again.

- **Guys who talk about other women.** If your date or boyfriend is talking about his ex or other women in general, it means he doesn't like you enough. Even if he talks negatively about them, it usually means he's not that into you, but is just using you to vent or be his therapist. Buyer beware, and Next! When a guy really likes you, he wants to talk about you!

- **Alcoholics, drug addicts, or any other kind of addict.** If your boyfriend drinks heavily or gets wasted all the time, buyer beware, what you see is what you get. He may sober up one day or he may not. You can ask him to go to Alcoholics Anonymous or check into rehab; you can join a support group to learn how to detach with love, but don't think any of that will necessarily change him. Some guys just cannot be changed. If your boyfriend has a debt problem or a sex addiction or a bad temper, buyer beware. He may get solvent and stop watching internet porn or he may always act this way. So either accept him and look the other way or break up.

- **Guys who have ulterior motives.** You make more money than he does and he asks you to pick up the bill. He seems to perk up when he finds out you live in a duplex two-bedroom, as he lives in his parents' basement. If you don't want to attract gold diggers or users, don't tell guys how much you make or spend money on them.

And if you don't want to attract guys who may be trying to use you for sex or to get over their ex-girlfriend or out of boredom, don't break *Rules* by sleeping with them too soon or acting like their therapist or agreeing to see them last minute. Doing *The Rules* weeds out guys who want to be with you for the wrong reasons.

- **Guys who get angry if they don't see you all the time or don't hear from you more often.** Sometimes a woman will wonder how to stick to the "seeing him only twice or three times a week" *Rule* or "wait four hours to text back" *Rule* when the guy is asking her out 24/7 and complaining that she doesn't call him back fast enough. She should nicely say she is busy and can't see or text him more often—and she doesn't need to give a reason. The guys who really like her will understand and be patient, but the guys who argue and complain that they can't get to know her without hearing from her and seeing her more are usually time wasters. Caitlin, a thirty-year-old PA, was dating a guy who would get angry if she didn't make time for him more often. She was so afraid that he would break up with her if she didn't see him when-ever he wanted that she gave into his demands. After two years of dating, Caitlin asked him, "Where is this going?" His answer: "I don't know yet." Not only had she spent a ton of time with him, but they had also vaca-tioned together and met each other's friends and fam-ily. Being compliant and showing a guy how compatible you are doesn't make him love you more or commit. She waited another six months and asked him again—but he said he still didn't know. See? When you give some guys an inch, they take a mile.

ou out for Saturday night. If a
plans with you on a weeknight,
ls are for guy friends, he may
t may not like you enough and
't see him during the week, as
l after a point. If he wants to
you out on serious dates. Text
y this week" so he is forced to
r Saturday night. If he doesn't,
oman in his life!

If you date a guy for nine
sn't ask to be exclusive or say
...then he is probably seeing other women. If
you met online and have been dating for several months,
check to see if his profile is still up. If it is, it's probably
not because he forgot to take it down or doesn't know
how, but because he's still dating other women, so buyer
beware! When a guy is ready to commit, the first thing
he says is "I don't want to date anyone else, so I'm taking
my profile down" and asks you to do the same. Depending on your age, if you have been dating a guy for two or
more years and he doesn't bring up the future, it is probably not on his mind. He may think you will date him
forever, so buyer beware! When you are ready, you will
need to nicely ask him, "Where do you see this going?"
and break up with him if he doesn't have concrete plans.

Without *The Rules*, women will rationalize giving buyer-
beware guys a second chance and spend the rest of the relationship being angry, hurt, or confused. We believe in nipping
it in the bud. If a guy is difficult in the first few months when

he is supposed to be charming and chivalrous, don't kid yourself. Buyer beware... be careful or move on! Of course, one woman's buyer beware is another woman's Mr. Right. You can't always help who you fall in love with, but *Rules* Girls don't put up with bad behavior!

Don't Be Self-Destructive by Dating Married, Unavailable, and Other Mixed-Messages Guys

AS WE WROTE in our first book, dating a married man is not only dishonest and wrong, but a sign of low self-esteem and desperation—and nothing a *Rules* Girl would ever do. It's also a complete waste of time as married men rarely leave their wives for the other woman. And even if they do leave, there is no guarantee that they will marry you, the home wrecker. And even if they do marry you, they will probably cheat on you too, so run the other way!

It used to be that the only way a guy could cheat was to go to a bar or come on to his secretary or coworker. Today's world has opened up new avenues, and cheating has never been easier.

Furthermore, social networking sites, online dating communities, text messaging, and e-mail have made inappropriate or fantasy relationships with unavailable men accessible at the stroke of a keyboard. Some women reconnect with high school or college sweethearts on Facebook, only to find out after a month of chatting that he is married and conveniently omitted his relationship status on his profile. Other women friend guys they meet at work or school on Facebook and end up in equally inappropriate or fantasy relationships with unavailable guys.

Natalie, a twenty-one-year-old college student, had a crush on her college professor, so she friended him on Facebook. He immediately accepted and was unprofessionally friendly; the relationship escalated quickly. They texted and messaged each other morning, noon, and night. Within weeks they were hooking up in hotel rooms near campus—they were having a torrid affair. He told her he was unhappily married and planning to leave his wife, who was not on Facebook and had no idea what was going on. He constantly complained about his wife when they were out on dates, giving Natalie false hope that he was gettable. In the beginning, he took her to fancy restaurants, but within a month they were eating Happy Meals in bed. By the second month, it was just sex, no dinner. This lack of courtship is typical when you sleep with a married man! He starts to treat you kind of like a hooker.

Natalie began complaining that she didn't see him enough—certainly never on weekends or important occasions. She asked him at least to take her out to dinner for her birthday. He said he would see what he could do, and then bailed on her at the last minute because his wife's sister was in town and he was "stuck." He said he would make it up to her and sent her cheap flowers. The following week Natalie was texting him almost nonstop, but getting no response. She messaged him on Facebook, "Where are you? What is going on?" He wrote back, "My wife is pregnant. I realized that I do love her and want to work things out. Sorry, but I can't see you anymore." He then blocked her on Facebook.

Natalie was devastated and didn't go to class for a week. She could barely get out of bed, much less study. She lost not only her self-respect, but also six months of her life to a cheater and a liar. And because she had isolated herself from her friends so as not to divulge her secret, she had no one to talk to when the relationship was over. Natalie was too embarrassed to tell anyone what happened, lest they judge her for having an affair.

This is a cautionary tale. Don't be Natalie! No matter how exciting such a relationship may seem at first, it never has a happy ending; the heartache always outweighs the clandestine dates and forbidden sex. When a woman tells us she is dating or in love with a married man and wants to know what the best way is to get him, we examine her dating history and other relationships to find out why she may be obsessed with unavailable men. Invariably, we find out that one or both of her parents were emotionally distant and that is all she knows. So no matter how unfulfilling her tryst with a married man may be, it's also comfortable and familiar. We tell women like this to break the self-destructive cycle by saying "Next!" and putting themselves out there to meet men who are truly available.

You might argue, "But he is so my look and type and I never meet anyone I like" or "Dating a married guy is better than being alone" or "He promised to leave his wife." If you find yourself making such excuses, tell the married guy to call you when he is separated and no longer living with his wife, and then don't give him the time of day—*no* communication—and get busy dating other people! You can easily waste years having sex in cheap hotels, believing in empty promises, and spending holidays alone while he's on vacation in Aruba with his family!

It's important to note that married men are not the only men who are unavailable. Sometimes a woman will reach out, asking us how to get the guy in her office who stares at her or the guy at the gym who always uses the treadmill next to her. "It's been three months, he looks at me, he flirts with me, but he never asks for my number…What do I do?"

Unfortunately, *nothing*! Sometimes guys like to flirt and are super friendly, but if they are not asking you out for coffee or drinks or a date, they might have a girlfriend. If a guy stares at you or even talks to you and flirts with you, but doesn't ask you out, it's a fantasy relationship. Don't try to move things along by sitting next to him or innocently suggest discussing your workout regimen over coffee. You will either get rejected immediately or create a relationship that was never supposed to happen and get rejected *later*. Nothing good will come of it, so just don't go there!

Sometimes a fantasy relationship begins with a guy friend who suspects you've always had a little crush on him. You've been hanging out a lot and then one day he asks if you want to try being more than friends. He might say he's always been attracted to you, but felt you were out of his league (first red flag!), or that he is shy and most women usually come on to him anyway (yeah, right!). He throws it all out there and wants to know if you are game. You say, "Sure, let's try it." You hook up, and then, just when you expected him to follow through, the relationship becomes completely confusing. He doesn't ask you out on dates, he just texts you last minute to hang out like he always did, or he invites you on a ski trip and you sleep together, but then he skips Valentine's Day. The relationship is fraught with mixed messages. He dips in and out of your life. You even joke with your girlfriends that he might be in the Witness Protection Program because you can never find him, especially on your birthday or New Year's Eve.

We call such men "mixed-messages" guys. They try to make you think that you are in a relationship and occasionally even talk about it, but their actions don't match up. When you call him out on his less than boyfriend-like behavior, he defends it by saying, "My last breakup was really bad, so I don't know if I can do this" or "I'm a mess right now" or he swears the florist screwed up the flowers he ordered that never came for your birthday. He has a long list of excuses, which a lot of women buy into. Then, just when you think you're through with him for good, he'll text, "How come we don't see each other more?" to rope you back in. Arggh! Mixed messages!

Naturally you are baffled and want to know what is going on. Don't be. *Nothing* is going on. Why does he bother at all? What's in it for him? We've had many consultations about mixed-messages guys and we've come to the conclusion that he might be getting back at an ex-girlfriend or all women in general; he had a love-hate relationship with his mother; or he's just bored and being with you here and there is fun for him like a sport or video game—whatever it is, he's not in love with you!

Sometimes these women argue that the guy is doing *The Rules* on them, but guys don't do *The Rules* on women—they just don't like them enough. We hate to break it to you, but there are no mixed messages when a guy likes you! Once a guy crosses over and suggests being more than friends but then doesn't follow through like a real boyfriend would, it's over. Next! The last thing you need is a confused guy texting and messaging you sporadically, giving you false hope. For all you know, he has four other women just like you waiting for him to finish whatever work project or emotional issue he's working on. He's not even married, but he's just as unavailable.

Remember, today's new technology has brought fantasy relationships to a whole new level of bad. A guy can text a girl sporadically, making her think he likes her or that they're in a relationship. He asks her out only when he wants to hook up, but she can't really complain that she never hears from him because he stays in touch electronically. He will send frivolous "what's up?" or "how was your weekend?" texts and instant message pretending to care about her, but it's really because he's bored and just keeping the relationship going so she is available when his dream girl is not or when he has nothing better to do. Many women fall for these guys under false pretenses. They waste years in on-again, off-again relationships, but we tell them there is no such thing. A relationship is either on with weekly dates or completely off! One of the reasons we wrote this book is to weed out these guys right away and prevent them from breaking your heart and wasting your time.

Stop Dating a Guy Who Cancels More than Once

WE SPENT *RULE* #22 discussing red flags in men's behavior and avoiding Mr. Wrong. But a guy who cancels a date more than once, unless it's a bona fide emergency, is such a buyer beware that we felt this behavior warranted its own chapter.

Women ask us all the time if it's okay to see a guy who canceled yet again and wants to reschedule. They tell us, "He just texted me that he got a flat tire and needs to take a rain check" or "He e-mailed to say that he can't meet me tonight because his friend invited him to a football game. What should I do?"

We are not trying to sound overly dramatic here, but canceling is the kiss of death! Of course we know that the world has become a more casual place and no one thinks twice about flip-flopping lunch appointments in an e-mail, rescheduling drinks in a group text, or canceling a training session with the touch of an iPhone!

But in *The Rules* world, canceling a date—unless there's a real emergency—is not to be taken lightly. A guy should be able to make a date with you and keep it, regardless of work, the weather, or whatever else is going on in his life. A date with you should be sacred. It should be written in ink, not in pencil.

A guy will come up with any excuse when he wants to break a date. He's sick, his parents are visiting, a former coworker just called to have drinks, or he suddenly has a deadline. Women will argue with us that his excuse is plausible and beg to be allowed to give him a second chance. But the truth is that men don't cancel because their stomach is upset or because work is crazy (on Saturday night?), or because they got last-minute tickets to a football game. What's more likely is that a guy will cancel because he's just not that into you or because the girl he *really* likes suddenly became available.

Unfortunately, a woman with a crush or in love will believe a guy's reasons for canceling because she wants so badly to make the relationship work. She lies to herself or looks the other way. But over time and through more cancellations and disappointments, she becomes a nervous wreck filled with insecurity and trust issues. In a healthy *Rules* relationship, a guy calls or texts every week for Saturday night dates; he does not cancel or skip a week, so the woman enjoys a feeling of stability and security. She can relax and go about her business.

Hannah, twenty-eight, met her boyfriend at a sports bar. Andrew, thirty, spoke to her first and they went out a week later for drinks. After that he asked her out for the following Saturday night by Wednesday. So far, so good. But then he texted her Friday morning that he had to cancel because a friend from out of town decided to visit him last minute, and then he canceled *again* two weeks later because he was coming down with a cold. We said, "Oh no, this is not good, it sounds suspicious." Hannah believed him, but we didn't. We said, "On a Saturday night? Can't he see his friend *any* other time during the weekend? A cold? Really? We just don't trust this guy; his excuses seemed a little lame. Doesn't he want to gaze into your blue eyes over dinner and possibly make out with you?"

Hannah respected what we had to say, but was so head over heels in love with Andrew that she continued to date him, hoping against hope that we were wrong. We didn't hear from her again until two years later when she e-mailed that she needed another consultation about Andrew. Hannah confessed that Andrew had broken up with her a couple of times because she was pressuring him to propose; he told her he couldn't even think about it until he got a promotion. Two months later he got his promotion and proposed with a ring and a wedding date. She was happy and relieved.

A month before the wedding, he told her he was having a "major panic attack about work" and went to a therapist who agreed with him that getting married was too stressful at that time and advised him not to go through with the wedding. Hannah was in shock. "WHAT??? Cancel our wedding? Break my heart? I have to call all the bridesmaids and guests and tell them the wedding's off? Lose ten thousand dollars in deposits?" Sadly, we weren't that surprised. Any guy who can cancel more than one date can cancel a wedding. But over time, Hannah had grown so accustomed to accepting Andrew's excuses that she didn't even comprehend the enormity of what had just happened. She wanted to know if the relationship was still salvageable! We told her to sell the ring and move on.

Of course, this situation rarely—if ever—happens to a *Rules* Girl! *Rules* Girls don't put up with guys who cancel more than once. *Rules* Girls don't have to feel angry, disappointed, betrayed, or have to make excuses for guys while trying to figure out what is really going on with them.

Kelly, a junior in college, told us that a guy she had been seeing for a few weeks texted her that he couldn't take her to a party on a Friday night because something had come up with his fraternity. It just didn't sound right. She argued that he wanted to be frat president one day. We told her not to message him back and to find someone else to go to the party with. Sure enough, a week later he broke up with Kelly and started dating someone else. A lame cancellation is usually the beginning of a breakup!

Jessica, thirty-two, was setting up a first drink date with a divorced guy with kids who found her on Match.com. An hour before they were supposed to meet, he e-mailed her to change the time from 5 p.m. to 8 p.m. because "work was busy." We told her we're not thrilled with this guy. While we were discussing the situation with her, he texted again that he just realized it was Parents' Night at his son's school. Could they reschedule for the following week? He added: "I owe you dinner now for ruining your night!" We told her now it was really over! But Jessica thought he was cute and wanted to give him a second chance. She texted back, "Okay, good luck tonight," even though we didn't think it was a good idea. Of course, he never contacted her again. What would possess a guy to make a date and break it and never reschedule? He probably met someone else he liked better. *Don't* try to figure it out. If he cancels, especially more than once, he just doesn't like you enough!

We are not making these stories up! In almost twenty years of private consultations, we have rarely seen a relationship work when the guy canceled more than once. In fact, we have interviewed hundreds of happily married *Rules* wives and all of them said that their husbands never canceled a date for any reason. Winter cold, heavy rain, client meetings, term papers, medical school, traffic, the Super Bowl, a family wedding... nothing stops a guy from seeing you if he likes you. If a guy cancels more than once, we suspect he will cancel again and again. Next!

Don't Sext or Send a Guy Anything You Wouldn't Want Him to Have If You Break Up

THE TERM "SEXTING" was coined years ago to describe the trend among teenage girls and young women of sending explicit or suggestive messages, photos, and videos of themselves scantily clad to guys on their cell phones. While these young women obviously think sexting is fun, cool, and innocent, it's actually foolish, inappropriate, and dangerous. If a sext gets around, you will be absolutely mortified and mocked!

Basics first: Anything you send electronically can be easily saved, forwarded, copied, or posted on Facebook, loaded onto YouTube, etc.—leaving you completely humiliated. With the push of a button, a guy can show his friends your sext describing your favorite sexual positions or your e-mail begging him to take you back after your breakup. Of course you think, "He's my boyfriend and would never do anything to hurt me." That may be true today, but what if you have a fight tomorrow? If he gets angry or he gets drunk, he might think about getting even by posting your private chats or private *parts* online! It's happened before and will happen again. It's one thing to be sexually playful one on one, but it's something completely different to have it paraded on the internet.

The *Rule* is: Before you write or send anything to a guy, ask yourself if you would be comfortable with his having it if you were no longer dating. If the answer is no, then *don't do it*! Never let your guard down or give a guy ammunition to hurt you. With everything being broadcast on the internet today, you just never know!

Besides the clear exposure and embarrassment factors, the whole idea of sexting is the opposite of *The Rules* on so many levels. Here are more reasons sexting is a bad idea:

- **If you are the one initiating sexts, you become the aggressor, showing a guy that you are not "light and breezy and busy."** Rather, you insinuate that you have nothing better to do than stand on your bed in a Victoria Secret push-up bra and thong and take photos. Not smart and not cool! But responding to sexts is not smart either, since they can be used against you.

- **You're not being mysterious and you're certainly not being hard to get**. You're telling him exactly what's on your mind: him and sex! Not only that, but you're also more or less implying that you want to *have* sex with him. It becomes too obvious that you like him too much. Would you bother spending countless hours sending him inappropriate or desperate messages and photos otherwise? We think not!

- **You are not being a *cyberspace* Creature Unlike Any Other—you're not showing any self-respect.** A cyberspace CUAO is private and discreet and even a little prudish. She doesn't use sexting or sex to get a guy. She lets a guy fall in love with her essence and soul, not just her body. She is the good girl who saves it for the right guy or at least a relationship. Remember, a CUAO has standards; she would not compromise her relationships and reputation. Sexting sends a completely decadent message—that you are open for business—and that's not what you want!

- **You run the risk of your message being misinterpreted or Photoshopped.** Even sexts sent in a flirty, innocent way can get into the wrong hands and come back to haunt you in a way you never predicted.

Kara, a junior in college, learned this lesson the hard way: She sexted a naked photo of herself to her boyfriend, Nick, a senior. When their relationship fizzled out after a few months because of Kara's fits of jealousy and neediness, Nick passed the photo on to a former friend of hers (key word: "former"), and from there it went viral. After receiving 2,500 page views, Kara was so mortified that she transferred to a community college and moved back in with her parents. She quit the varsity track team, left her sorority sisters, and drove around in dark sunglasses and a baseball cap. Don't let this kind of embarrassment happen to you. *Rules* Girls are too smart and too classy for sexting!

Don't Accept Booty Calls or Meaningless Hookups

TWENTY-FIVE OR EVEN fifteen years ago, before Black-Berrys and iPhones, booty calls were hardly an issue at all. After all, how would a guy even find someone to hook up with in a matter of seconds in the middle of the night? Unless he just stumbled onto her, how would he know what bar or party she was at? We're not saying booty calls never happened, we're just saying it was a lot more difficult to make them happen. If a guy called a girl's house for sex at 2 a.m., he would wake up her parents or her roommate, so it didn't happen a lot.

Flash forward: Today, every girl has a GPS chip in her! Late-night hookups have never been easier or more rampant. Guys can reach out to girls anywhere, anytime. We know girls don't turn off their cell phones when they go to sleep so as not to miss any late-night texts—they sleep with them on their chests or next to their pillows. Smartphones have replaced teddy bears! All it takes is "where r u?" or "what r u up 2?" or "let's meet up!" Arrangements are very easily made.

So what is *The Rule* for booty calls? Simple: no answer! Ignore it! Delete it! If you get a late-night text saying, "what r u doing right now?" or "wanna hang out?" don't even write back, "too tired" or "no thanks" or anything else. Most guys will try to manipulate or shame you into meeting them through the flurry of time-wasting texts that will ensue. If you write back at all, chances are you will end up going to his place, having sex, getting hurt when he doesn't text you until the next hookup, and ultimately regretting it. So don't dignify booty-call texts with an answer, and definitely don't waste time worrying that you are being rude. It's rude of *him* to text you so late. If he really liked you, he would have made plans ahead of time, not at 2 a.m. for 2:15 a.m. Guys who like you think about you in advance. A booty-call invitation is an insult. Don't feel flattered and don't be afraid you are offending him by not answering. He doesn't deserve a reply.

The bottom line is that a booty call will not lead to real dates, romance, or the closeness you crave. It may start out full of excitement, but it will leave you feeling empty, hurt, and damaged. Even if you're not looking for a husband right now, you want to be treated with respect and keep a good reputation. Maybe you're thinking, "I can't help it. I like him and I think he likes me" or "I don't care if it leads to a relationship" or "It's okay if I don't hear from him again" or "Whatever happens, I can handle it." Or you're thinking, "I'm a big girl now, so I can do whatever I want" or even "What's the big deal?" These are all rationalizations that even the smartest young women buy into. But the truth is that booty calls simply are not good for you. It's not a question of right or wrong or a moral issue—booty calls are bad because they don't work. They don't lead to dates, a healthy relationship, or *any* relationship at all. No matter what you tell yourself, you *do* care if you don't hear from him again and you *do* want to be called, texted, wanted, and, most importantly, respected the day after you are with a guy. That is why you are thinking about going through with the booty call at all! Rather than appreciating that the latest technology lets guys get in touch with them so easily, many young women actually feel flattered—"Oh, he's texting me at 2 a.m., I must be on his mind!"

Alcohol and drugs can play a big part in such hookups. Jessica, a college sophomore, has never gone on a booty call sober because she makes poor choices only when she is wasted—yet another reason to limit yourself to one or two drinks when you go out, as we strongly suggest in *Rule #21*. You need a clear head to turn down a good-looking athlete or the VP of marketing late at night. These guys are used to girls throwing themselves at them—they rarely, if ever, hear the word "no." They can probably talk you into meeting up with them for a late-night tryst, so it's important not to give them the chance to. Being under the influence will make it more difficult for you to ignore them.

Another factor contributing to the frequency of booty calls, especially in college, is proximity. There are so many house parties, fraternity parties, post-bar parties—but you're never too far from home. Clearly, you have to exercise a lot of self-control not to hook up meaninglessly. If you are serious about turning down booty calls, you might want to find other *Rules* Girls to support you who you can reach out to if you're feeling weak. Maybe you can seek her out at a party if you feel tempted, or ask her to keep an eye on you. Sometimes good girls make bad choices when it comes to men!

Lauren, twenty, comes from a good family—she was a Girl Scout and churchgoer; her father is a lawyer and her mother is a PTA mom. But Lauren started going on booty calls in the second semester of her freshman year. She felt desperate to have a boyfriend; without a guy in her life, she felt awkward and lonely. She thought if she hooked up with some frat guy, it would lead to something more and she would feel pretty and popular. She rationalized that she was liberal, she was a feminist, it was the twenty-first century, and she could do whatever she wanted. After all, she figured, what's the worst that could happen?

An Unexpected Side Effect

Booty-call girls might be breaking their own hearts by chasing after emotionally unavailable guys, but they also tend to break one of the most sacred laws of womanhood: sisters before misters. When a girl drops everything to jump into a guy's bed, her friends are usually affected, too. Sadly, we see it all the time. A girl who blows off movie night because "he asked if I wanted to hang out." A girl who ditches dinner plans because "he texted me this time, and he never texts me." A girl who shows up super late to her BFF's birthday because "he's really cute! Why can't you just be happy for me?!" Dropping your friends for a guy every time just sends them the message that they don't matter (and sends him the message that he's the only one who does). Best not to burn your friends too many times, or there won't be anyone there when your booty call drops *you*.

—*Rules Daughters*

Lauren introduced herself to Brian at a party, and he was more than happy to sleep with her that night. But the late-night hookup never led to any dates, let alone a relationship. When she reached out to us, we told her that it was not going to go anywhere with Brian and to stop seeing him, but she wouldn't listen. He texted her about once a week to hang out at his place, always at 2 a.m. after the bars closed or after he had sometimes taken out another girl who wouldn't sleep with him—booty-call texts. Brian was either drinking or drunk. Lauren had convinced herself that he really liked her, but when she turned Brian down for the first time, he yelled, cursed, and belittled her. When he tried to shame her into hooking up with him by saying, "What, you're too good for me?" it was the last straw. He made her feel horrible.

If you really want to stop going on booty calls and stop meaningless hookups, stop lying to yourself. Every one of these hookups starts with some kind of lie that "this time will be different" or "this time I won't care if he doesn't ask me out" or "this is how I will get my ex back" or "this will make him see how good I am in bed and like me and ask me out."

Missy, twenty-five, had a much worse experience than Lauren. She traveled a lot for work and often felt lonely in the downtime between her meeting-filled days. On one such business trip, she hooked up with a guy she met at the hotel bar and fell asleep in his room that night. He decided to take a naked photo of her and post it online; everyone saw it. She tried to remove it, but as you can imagine, once it is out there, it's not so easy to take down. Missy was hysterical and is still working on getting over feeling violated. But this experience scared her into stopping her drunk and careless behavior. Unfortunately, sometimes something awful or embarrassing has to happen to wake a girl up and make her realize that what she is doing is not only unproductive, but also downright destructive. Missy never went on a booty call again. With our help, she is now dating nice guys who respect her and ask her out on dinner dates. We told her to move on like it never happened and not to let the incident haunt her, because any man who loves her will not care. Looking back, Missy could not believe she ever accepted such crumbs from men. She now realizes that any man who tries to see you last minute in the middle of the night will treat you barely better than a hooker. A man will treat you the way you let him!

When a guy doesn't care about you, he will do anything for a laugh or a thrill, even at your expense. Not hearing from a guy again is bad enough, but being taunted by a booty call is a whole new level of scary. Your reputation and even education or career can be severely damaged in a nanosecond, so think twice about hooking up with someone who isn't crazy about you or someone you don't trust.

Many girls who engaged in casual hookups in college find themselves repeating the same behavior in their mid- to late twenties. But why would it just stop? Bad habits are hard to break. Going back to casual sex is like going back to cigarettes—you crave something to help you stop feeling low or lonely, whether it's a substance or a sex partner. The more you do it, the harder it is to stop. If you're sleeping around at any time in your life, *just stop*. It's stupid and it's only going to stay with you. Instead of working on a stable, constructive *Rules* relationship, you'll be answering booty-call texts in the middle of the night. Sure, it is bad enough to accept a booty call at eighteen, but at twenty-eight, it's self-destructive because the stakes are so much higher. You have a job, rent to pay, and many other responsibilities. There is less room for error, and it's just not smart to be in relationships that are totally physical and with no future. Why?

Because at twenty-eight and older, most women are looking for meaningful relationships with men they can love and trust.

Furthermore, it doesn't matter who the guy is—booty calls are *never* good for you. Alexa, twenty-six, was casually hooking up with her ex-boyfriend, reasoning that it was okay because she knew him. She was going out to bars and parties almost every night, meeting no one. She ended up getting in touch with her ex and going to his place because, after all, he wasn't a stranger. She hoped it would lead to their getting back together. This arrangement went on for a year after he had broken up with her before she realized that the relationship was going nowhere. It *never* works when you have sex with a guy you want a relationship with who doesn't feel the same way. In fact, ex-boyfriends are sometimes the worst offenders because they often lead you to believe that they want to get back together ("It's just that right now is a bad time") when all they really want is sex. Girls end up wasting time and living in the past or having a fantasy relationship instead of moving on and meeting new guys.

It's not that bad things always happen on booty calls, but that sometimes *nothing* happens, which *is* what's bad. You don't go the extra mile to meet someone new; it doesn't lead to a long-term relationship—it's just instant gratification and then pain. Waste of time! *The Rules* are all about long-term gratification, not a quick night of fun followed by pain and regret. When you're a *Rules* Girl, you know what a date is and you know how you deserve to be treated. It's not just about ignoring late-night invitations, but also about holding out for a healthy *Rules* relationship.

How do guys feel about girls who go on booty calls? We

polled hundreds of guys in college and beyond. Here's what some had to say:

"In college, everybody talks. And with cell phones, word travels fast."

"No guy will respect her. They'll think, 'She's too easy... I don't have to work that hard to see her' and move on to someone else. Or if they do text or call again, it's just to do it again."

"They are easy—not girlfriend material. No one wants to date someone who has been with all their friends. I hope these girls are gone when I wake up. I would never touch her sober."

"It's bad. A lot of times it's the girl texting guys at 2 a.m. and it's never to talk, only to hook up. She will write, 'hey what are you up to' or 'where are you' and my friends and I will laugh because we know she means, 'I want to have sex.'"

"One girl sent me and my friend the same exact text saying her roommate was out so she had the room to herself, but we were sitting next to each other when we got it. Neither of us went obviously."

"Advice? No guy wants to date a 2 a.m. booty-call girl. They want to date the girl who won't come over."

"I think it's a perfect situation for a guy who's not looking for a relationship. You have a sex buddy who's more than willing to sleep with you and more than likely thinks you are serious about her, if not now, then one day."

Wait before Sleeping with a Guy

WE LIVE IN a sex-crazed society, where songs about one-night stands and S&M play all day long, and TV shows portray young women dressed up like hookers carrying condoms in their Chanel bags. Teen pregnancy is always on the news in some capacity, and nineteen-year-olds have sex tapes!

It's a sex culture, all right. But the fact that other women are buying into it now more than ever before doesn't mean you should! You are a *Rules* Girl: you have self-esteem, standards, and boundaries. So when is it sensible for a *Rules* Girl to have sex?

Your first time is a big deal, so you shouldn't rush to get it over with or be with the wrong guy. Ideally, you should be in some sort of a relationship with a guy who is into you, who cares about you, who is kind to you, and who wants to cuddle afterward—not someone who treats you like a notch on his belt and can't get away fast enough. You don't want your first time to be unpleasant or something you long to forget. We think you should be at least eighteen, and wait as long as you can—ideally a year into the relationship. If you are older, you should still wait at least three months (or twelve consecutive dates—a lot of time spent together). In any case, make sure you trust him and feel comfortable with him.

A *Rules* Girl makes a guy wait to help him fall in love with her, her soul, and her essence—not just her body. The longer you wait to have sex, the more he can court you, plan romantic things together, and dream about you. Guys will treat you better and respect you more if you don't give sex away too soon. As we keep saying over and over again, guys love a challenge and don't appreciate anything that comes too easily, especially sex! Women who take off their clothes on date one or even date two or three are not acting hard to get; they are the opposite of Creatures Unlike Any Other. These girls run the risk of getting dumped or becoming the late-night booty-call girl because it's obvious how easily they'll give it up.

It used to be that HIV, sexually transmitted diseases, and getting pregnant were the only risks for sexually active women. These are still dangers you'll face, but now, there are a whole host of other pitfalls waiting for women who succumb too soon. A guy can humiliate you by planting cameras in the room and posting your dalliance online or e-mailing it to everyone. He can tell everyone about your night together and watch how quickly the rumor mill turns with text messages and Twitter. Sleeping with a guy you just met is a really bad idea. If he doesn't know you well, he probably doesn't care about you and won't think twice about hurting you. Conversely, the more he gets to know you, the safer he will make you feel.

When you do decide you want to sleep with a guy, first ask yourself if you truly believe he will call or text you afterward. It's a terrible idea to hook up with someone you don't think you'll hear from again. Even if you think you "don't care," that's not necessarily how you'll feel the next morning or next week. Women tell us all the time that they "don't care" if the guy just wanted sex and nothing more. They say things like "We locked eyes and we knew it was going to happen; we just had to do it." They convince themselves that they are capable of feeling like a man when it comes to sex, but the next morning they are compulsively checking their phones and are completely heartbroken when they don't hear from the guy. Even *Sex and the City*'s Samantha Jones fell for a guy or two!

It's always better to wait until you have an emotional connection before a physical one so you don't get hurt. Women want to bond with a guy, snuggle, and hear words such as "like" and "love" and "exclusive." They want security and a sense of togetherness. For guys, sex can be more mechanical. When it's over, they often get up, get dressed, and go to work, no problem. No matter what you anticipate you'll feel, it's always the same. Most women are hardwired to desire emotional intimacy and invariably end up hurt when they act under any other pretense.

Also crucial: ensure that you have the right motives. Don't use sex to trap a guy into a relationship. Don't act lovey-dovey as he is putting on his socks and say, "So when am I going to hear from you?" or text him later, "Where is this relationship going now that we have slept together?" Sex is not an excuse to have a relationship talk or all-night instant-messaging chat. He doesn't owe you anything emotionally just because you've had sex. Going into the act with this mind-set is manipulative and will usually backfire. Sometimes a woman's obvious expectations or demands that sex bring more closeness and familiarity can send a guy running.

Now, some women say they would never sleep with a guy on the first date, but are open to everything else: they let guys put handcuffs on them and have oral sex and think that doesn't count. But it does. When we say make a guy wait, we mean no more than casual kissing on the first date. On the second date, you can French kiss if he wants to. On the third or fourth date, you can make out a little more. By the time he wants to sleep with you, if you feel it's not the right time yet, you can absolutely say, "I'd like to, but I'm not ready." If he gets angry or threatens to stop seeing you, then he's not the guy for you. Don't let any man pressure you into sleeping with him too soon!

Other women carry this "make him wait for sex" *Rule* to the extreme. We don't suggest you necessarily make a man wait until you are married. Of course, if you are religious or have other beliefs that support abstinence, we respect that. It is important not to be a tease: if you are not planning to sleep with him for six months or a year for whatever reason, it's only fair to tell him so he can decide whether he wants to wait. Sometimes making a guy wait *too* long can attract guys who are not really into sex at all. He may be relieved because he has a low sex drive or prefers porn to intimacy or is just not that into you. How will you know if you are sexually compatible if you wait until you are married? Sex is an important part of any relationship—we just believe it should be approached with caution.

But here's the tricky part of this *Rule*: Let's say you're more into sex than the guy is. You feel he is going too slowly (only kissing you on the fifth date) and you want to speed things up. Should you make a move? Absolutely not! If you initiate anything physical, you are creating a situation in which you are the aggressor, which might make you feel self-conscious in other parts of the relationship. It's hard to feel desired and secure when you are doing most of or all the work. Sex should be treated like any other part of your relationship—he should make the first move and make you feel wanted. If he is not sexually aggressive enough for you, then maybe he is not the right guy for you.

Conversely, withholding sex to punish a guy is not good either. When something in the relationship is not going their way, some women's impulse is to get even by denying a guy sex. We are totally against that tactic. Once you've had sex with a guy, there is no going back—the tone has been set. The best way to deal with a bump in the relationship is to see him less, pull back, and be suddenly busy. *The Rules* are more emotional than physical. He needs to feel that you are slipping away and that he may lose you. So see him less and don't always answer his messages, but if you *do* see him, you should continue to sleep with him if you have already. Otherwise, he will think you are spiteful.

No matter when you decide you're ready to have sex with a guy, be smart and practice it safely. Don't let a guy convince you in the heat of the moment that it's okay not to use a condom "just this once." If you are on birth control and in a committed, exclusive relationship, ask him to get tested for STDs. You can even ask to see the doctor's report, as some guys will lie about getting tested. If you have any doubts whatsoever, use a condom. *Rules* Girls play it safe and take care of themselves!

Go to the Gym and Other *Rules* for Looking Good at Every Age

DATING IS HARD enough! If you want to make it even harder, just put on fifteen, twenty, or fifty pounds. Like it or not, we live in a thin-obsessed world where guys have their pick of girls, so most prefer a thin girlfriend, not an over-weight one. By thin, we don't mean anorexic, just slender and fit. The clinical definition of overweight is 10 percent more than your recommended body weight. So if you are 150-plus pounds when you should be 135, you are technically over-weight. Of course, what guys want should not be the only reason to look good—eating right is not about being a size 8 or 10—you want to look good for you, for your confidence and self-esteem. But since this is a dating book, not a diet book, what guys think counts as well. Besides, when you get in shape for yourself, you can be a confident Creature Unlike Any Other—your feeling good is attractive, too!

We polled dozens of college-aged guys as well as guys twenty-five and older, and they all said the same thing. They do not want to go out with an overweight girl. Call it sexist, unfair, or shallow, but it's the truth! An average-looking slender girl has a better chance of attracting a guy than a very pretty overweight girl. Here are some comments from guys:

"There is nothing sexy or appealing about a very over-weight girl."

"Would I go out with an overweight girl? No. I would just be her friend."

"If she's fifteen pounds heavier because she got chunky on a semester abroad in Spain, I would go out with her because she'll probably lose the weight. But if she's been very overweight her whole life, then no."

"An overweight girl is thought of as someone who doesn't even try. Just about everyone works out—why can't she? "

"If a girl doesn't like herself enough to diet and exercise, why should I?"

"I won't date anyone who won't wear a two-piece bathing suit!"

If you are not happy with how you look, you might want to consider doing something to change that. We are not trying to make you feel bad—and please don't get upset as you are reading this—we just want to be honest about how your appearance can affect you socially. We want to explain why eating right and exercising can sometimes make the difference between going out on a date and sitting home alone on a Saturday night.

Courtney, twenty-nine, blew up from a size 10 to a size 16 in her freshman year and also blew any chance of dating the cute guys she had crushes on. She was nervous about school and turned to food to calm herself down. She ate huge meals in the dining hall, candy bars in between classes, and late-night pizza. She had no dates. The only time she was with a guy was when they were drunk and she met them in their room after a party at 2 a.m. They didn't even take her to the party—she was just the late-night hookup girl. All the guys she hung out with would say, "You're really nice, but I just like you as a friend" or "I don't like you that way" or "I like you like a sister." She was so depressed she could barely study, so she ended up having to transfer to a less academically competitive school. But Courtney didn't want to start at a new school being overweight, so she started working out and lost thirty-five pounds over the summer. In fact, she met her first real boyfriend at the gym. Her weight loss, combined with the confidence it brought her, changed her dating status for good.

Nikki, thirty, told us that when she was in college, she couldn't get from lunch to dinner without stopping at the vending machines. She said her self-esteem was "in the toilet" and she couldn't get the cute guys she really wanted, so she took what she could get. One guy who liked Nikki actually told her roommate to tell her that he would go out with her if she lost twenty-five pounds, so she did. But she would take off the weight and then put it right back on. She was a yo-yo dieter. After graduation, Nikki finally lost her extra weight for good through a strict low-carbohydrate food plan and group support. She realized that she had been using food to deal with school stress and social anxiety. By putting food in its proper place, she started dating and met the man who is now her husband.

Stress. Workload. Social anxiety. Low self-esteem. Not having a boyfriend. A bad breakup. Depression. Fear. Feeling overwhelmed. Feeling not good enough, not smart enough, or not popular enough are some of the most common reasons why women of all ages binge on food. Rationalizing that you are young and have the rest of your life to lose weight and exercise is also common, especially in college. Add to that an unlimited dining hall menu, vending machines, snack bars, and deliveries at any hour—and you have a recipe for disaster. Experts say if you want to know why you use food the way you do, the answer will reveal itself if you simply stop overeating! Underneath the food are usually negative feelings such as anger, jealousy, fear, anxiety, or self-hatred that you want to make disappear or medicate with Oreos.

Find a food plan that works for you. Whatever food plan or program you choose, realize that you are going to replace food with something better, be it exercise, a new hobby or interest, dating, a spiritual way of life, or all of the above! When you are not overeating or hating yourself, you will have more time and energy to make friends, do your work, and, of course, date.

Obviously, there is no shortage of diet programs and theories out there. We think half the battle is changing the way you eat. The other half is changing the way you think. Instead of thinking that fun is a hot fudge sundae, you should think that fun is fitting into your favorite jeans and being asked out by a guy you think is cute. Instead of thinking that you can eat whatever you want now and work it off tomorrow, you should think, "No dessert now and hot body sooner rather than later." Instead of thinking that nothing beats donuts dipped in butter cream, think nothing beats being in a bikini on the beach. Think long term. Being disciplined with food will help you be disciplined with dating, work or school assignments, time, money, and everything else. Dieting and *The Rules* are very similar in that not eating and not texting right away, for example, are both about delayed gratification.

Weight gain, not looking good, not feeling good, and even

not having a boyfriend are only short-term consequences. Long term, overweight women can lose a whole decade of dating. Why? There are a ton of guys to meet in college, but afterward, the pool of eligible bachelors dwindles drastically. So if you didn't have any boyfriends in college because you weren't happy with your body, then you may not start dating until your twenties and or even thirties when you finally take dieting, exercise, and your health seriously. Your friends might be engaged or married with children and you will first start going on dates or joining dating websites. Being overweight can make most women depressed and want to chase guys and break other *Rules*, too. Some of our clients in their thirties and forties missed out on having boyfriends and sex when they were younger because they were too busy hating their bodies. They had to learn everything later in life. Don't let this happen to you!

Diet Tips

Here are some of our favorite tried-and-true diet tips for college and beyond:

- **Don't be afraid to use a digital scale and measuring cups to portion out your food; it will keep you honest.** It's too easy to lie to yourself and eat three servings instead of one when you are upset about a guy or overwhelmed with work or just plain tired.

- **If you choose to count calories, remember that not all calories are equal.** For example, a 100-calorie apple is more nutritious and filling than a 100-calorie cookie or 100-calorie can of light beer, so make smart choices.

- **If restaurants throw you off your diet, tell the waiter or waitress to skip the bread basket.** Order a salad instead of a fattening appetizer like mozzarella sticks. Order grilled fish, chicken, or meat (nothing fried) and vegetables instead of a starch. Order fruit instead of dessert and drink diet soda or tonic water instead of the more calorific regular soda and/or mind-altering alcohol.

- **When you go to parties or weddings where food will be served, eat before you leave home so you are not ravenous or tempted when you arrive.** That way you can fill up on something healthy. Eating before you go will also free you up to mingle, dance, and be approached by a cute guy instead of being glued to the buffet table or snack bowl at the bar.

- **When you are working, keep healthy snacks like baby carrots and apples around so you are full and don't hit the vending machines or order something unhealthy.** Even Jackie Kennedy Onassis carried carrot sticks in her purse to snack on when she was hungry! Her healthy habits in no way diminished her stature as First Lady and fashion icon, so you shouldn't be embarrassed to do the same.

- **Learn to eat healthy with a friend.** Make sure it's someone you trust and someone with the same point of view as you. You can call her when you feel like bingeing or when you have a feeling or problem that you might normally eat over. You can send her your food and exercise plan so you are held accountable for the good choices you are making.

- **Keep a journal or a log with your daily food intake, as well as your thoughts.** Writing down what you eat will help you stay honest with yourself. Writing down how you feel or what is bothering you will help you get it out so you don't cover it up with food.

- **Add up how much money you are spending on binge food,** including pizza deliveries, gourmet restaurants, and ice cream runs—not to mention having to buy more clothes because nothing fits. Doing so will help cut any denial about how much bingeing is costing you. If it's $10 or more a day, that's $10 you could be spending on healthy habits like manicures and pedicures or going to see a movie. Also add up the emotional cost of being overweight—missed classes and bad grades from being hung over from late-night binges, being the last to have a boyfriend, not having a date to the prom or sorority dance, etc.

- **Be careful about low-fat or low-calorie foods from health food stores or frozen-yogurt places.** These treats are usually filled with sugar or sugar substitutes—they do not offer the same nutritional value that real foods do and can actually be quite calorific. These fake foods must be eaten in small portions or not at all. They have sneaky ingredients like dextrose and sucrose and are sometimes even addictive.

- **Don't try crash diets, juice fasts, starvation, or anything extreme.** Don't binge and purge or take laxatives. Don't have black coffee and a cigarette for breakfast. Most diet organizations recommend a weight-reducing food plan consisting of three meals a day (1,200 to 1,500 calories) with or without a snack or two.

- **Don't read, study, watch TV, talk on the phone, or do anything else while *eating*.** Eventually you will associate food with that activity and feel hungry whenever you are doing it. Food is not a companion or a recreational activity. When you eat your meals, sit down at the table; once you've finished, the kitchen closes and you move into another room or on to another activity. Separate eating from living!

- **Weigh yourself once a week or once a month—not every day and certainly not three times a day.** Don't become a slave to the scale. If you gain a pound or two because of your period or water weight, you might end up feeling like your healthy eating plan is not working and use that as an excuse to console yourself with food. Also, remember that weight comes off quickly the first month or two of a diet and then slows down, so don't expect to drop ten pounds a month every month! Remember that healthy eating is a way of life. Don't focus too much on weight loss; instead, focus on the fact that you are taking care of yourself and feel better now than when you were bingeing—not only that, but your clothes fit better and guys are paying more attention to you, too.

Julia, thirty-two, gained twenty-five pounds after a really bad breakup. She desperately wanted to get fit again and start dating, but didn't know where to begin. Join a gym? Buy a treadmill? Run at the local high school? Join a matchmaking service? Put up an online profile? She couldn't decide. We gave Julia a food plan and told her to walk once around the block. We told her it was a great start and even though it wasn't much, she'd start to feel the benefits of getting physical activity. The next day Julia walked two blocks, and then ten, and then a mile. Three months later she e-mailed us that she had lost fifteen pounds and had signed up to run in a half marathon. She also met a cute guy when she joined a runners' club and they are now engaged. We are big believers in baby steps. Make a decision to do something, start somewhere, and see what happens!

Exercise Tips

Let's face it, exercise doesn't appeal to everyone. It can be hard, repetitious, and even boring! But exercise curbs your appetite, speeds up weight loss, tones your body, and releases endorphins—all great things! Sometimes it can be your best medicine. We've had clients who have started seeing a therapist and asked for an antidepressant. After consulting with us and going on a sensible diet with a workout plan, the depression lifted and they didn't even think about taking medication. Between academic or professional and social pressures, you need some kind of release; the endorphins you get from exercise can improve your mood and your whole outlook!

We asked a few personal trainers for their comments and suggestions on finding the best fitness plan for yourself. Here's what they had to say:

- **Determine what time of day is best for you to work out.** "I have one client who is a morning person. She works at home. If she doesn't exercise at 7 a.m., she never does. I told her to put on her sneakers as soon as she gets out of bed and turn on the treadmill. If she turns on her computer first and gets busy with e-mails, she just never gets around to it."

- **Make yourself responsible for exercise.** "Some of my clients hate to exercise more than life itself, so I don't give them an option not to. They are accountable to show up to our appointment." If you don't want to pay for a trainer, make plans to meet a friend or two in a class—if they don't show up, just exercise anyway!

- **One type of exercise is usually not enough.** You need both cardio and weight training. So try to mix it up. Go for a run and then do weights or take an aerobics class that combines cardio and weights. But don't feel you have to lift heavy weights—you can do more repetitions of lighter weights instead. Whatever you do, you have to sweat to get endorphins. No pain, no gain!

- **Do what you like—otherwise you won't do it!** There are so many different activities to try, from running to yoga to Pilates to biking, swimming, jumping rope, tennis, boxing, figure skating, Zumba dance classes. Mix it up and find what's best for you; otherwise you will get bored or frustrated and stop.

While dating is easier when you look good and feel good, we don't believe in waiting until you have the perfect body to go to singles events or get on an online dating site. Your life should not stop because you are not at your goal weight or in your goal jean size. You should be working on yourself *while* dating, not waiting for perfection. In the meantime, know how to look like your best self; as you progress with weight loss and exercise, your confidence will increase and that will work wonders for your dating life.

Fitting In Fitness

Between classes, internships, and keeping up with the social scene, daily gym time is usually the first thing to go in our busy schedules. But as our moms keep reminding us, staying in shape only gets harder with age, so it's important to make fitness a habit now before we're battling jiggly arms in our forties. Even with everything we have to get done, there is *always* some opportunity to fit in a workout during the day. Joining a local sports team will guarantee some extra cardio every week, or if you have some free time between classes, jump onto the elliptical or stationary bike for just twenty minutes or so—you can even bring a textbook to study if you need to multitask. You can make simple but effective decisions, like choosing the stairs over the elevator, or walking to campus instead of taking the shuttle bus. Whatever you can do to stay in shape will help you in the end, and it'll be worth it when you're rocking your favorite sleeveless shirts and short shorts. More importantly, exercising will help give you mental clarity, confidence, and a feeling of self-worth.

—*Rules Daughters*

Wait for a Guy to Follow You on Twitter First and Rarely Return Tweets

IF YOUR ROLE models for Twitter are singers, actresses, and reality stars, think again! Celebrities can tweet all they want—they are promoting and selling their TV shows, movies, songs, images, and products. For them, it's business; they tweet all day and try to gain as many followers as possible. Even if they're tweeting about their mundane daily business, people are fascinated! But if you are not famous, you need *Rules* for Twitter so you don't ruin your relationship by coming off as an oversharer or a stalker. Twitter is designed to give people access and information, so *Rules* Girls have to be especially careful with this medium of communication.

If you're going to use it, here are our tips for how to do so *and* still follow *The Rules*:

- **Keep your Twitter account protected, meaning you have to approve your followers.** That way you can keep track of everyone you're broadcasting to—including your crush! Not to mention, this privacy is smart in the workplace and for general safety.

- **Don't follow a guy on Twitter unless he follows you first.** And even then, wait about 24 to 48 hours to accept his request so you don't seem obsessed with him *or* with Twitter. Remember, you are happy and busy, not a junkie!

- **Don't respond to any of his open timeline tweets.**

- **If he sends you an @ reply, you can respond—but do so rarely!** If and when you do, be sure to write less than he did and avoid creating a continuing conversation.

- **Avoid tweeting every five minutes.** Once every day or so is enough. You have a life—and the whole world doesn't need constant updates on it on Twitter!

Foursquare

We all agree that mystery is a must when attracting the opposite sex, and what's the ultimate mystery killer? Location check-ins. Whether it's on Facebook or Twitter, broadcasting everywhere you go destroys the mystique that all these *Rules* have helped you to build, giving a guy unlimited insight into all the questions he should be trying to figure out on his own. What do you do in your free time? "Jamie checked in at the mall." What do you look for in a guy? "Jamie checked in at the midnight showing of *Twilight: Breaking Dawn*." The secrets to your beauty? "Jamie checked in at Downtown Facial Waxing Clinic." (Although we *really* hope no girls out there check in at the waxing salon!) Checking in is the ultimate mystery killer. *Rules* Girls just don't use it!

—*Rules Daughters*

- **Don't tweet anything mundane or anything negative (just like with Facebook status updates).** No one wants to hear that you are "walking the dog" or "had a bad week at work." Your tweets should be important, newsworthy, witty, or uplifting. "Training for the Race for Life" is a great example.

- **Don't tweet about love songs or chick flicks, because it shows too much interest in relationships.** You want to seem like you are interested in politics, sports, and the world in general, not just guys!

- **Don't tweet anything about your relationship. Period!**

- **Use hashtags carefully.** Be aware of the conversation you are joining, and make sure you are not propelling anything clichéd or non-*Rules*-y in any way.

- **If you find yourself tweeting too much or tweeting the wrong things, you should cancel your account.** It's more important to do it right than it is just to be on it!

Don't Date Indefinitely without a Commitment!

IF YOU'RE IN college or graduate school or have been dating someone casually or for just a few months, this chapter may not apply to you. But at a certain point in your life, you're no longer interested in relationships just for fun and entertainment. You want love and commitment—and why shouldn't you? Why spend Saturday nights and holidays alone when you can spend them with a significant other who gets you and wants to be with you?

Even if you are not looking to get married right now, you still want to be in a relationship that isn't a waste of your time. You should be subtly looking for clues about whether the guy sees a future so you are not blindsided if he decides he doesn't want to be exclusive or doesn't propose. Has he said, "I don't want to see anyone else?" Did he change his profile to say "in a relationship" on Facebook and/or post photos of both of you together or as his default photo? Has he used the word "love"? Has he invited you to be his date to a wedding or mentioned his nieces or nephews? All these are signs that he is serious about you and you might be headed for the altar one day.

Conversely, when your friend gets engaged, does he get awkward or quiet? Does he comment negatively on his friends' relationships that seem serious? Does he pose broad and confusing questions, such as "What *is* love?" or "What's so great about marriage?" Does he avoid talking about the future? When a client's relationship is not working out, one of the first questions we ask in a consultation is "Does he mention the 'M' word?" Most times the answer is no—he will happily talk about cars, sports, current events—anything but marriage. If that is the case with your guy, don't be surprised if he doesn't want to be exclusive or ultimately doesn't want to marry you. This cavalier attitude about commitment is especially prevalent in college, where most guys are not interested in a long-term relationship. They just want to study, have fun, and try new things—like being with a blonde, a brunette, and a redhead in the same semester! Even guys who are shy and not players are not looking to settle down at twenty or twenty-two.

Assuming the guy you are dating is saying all the right things, how do you get him to commit? If it's a *Rules* relationship, it should not be painful for him to commit. He should be happy about it! He loves you and wants to spend the rest of his life with you, right? You just have to help him start "the rest of his life." If it was a *Rules* beginning (he spoke to you first or contacted you through your online dating profile) but then you broke *Rules* (hung out with him constantly and texted him at all hours), he may not be so eager to make it official because he is getting all the benefits of marriage *without* a ring and a wedding. If that is the case, you need to pull back so that he feels like he is losing you before you lower the boom and bring up the future. Get busy at work, go away for a weekend with girlfriends, or text him back progressively less quickly. If it was never a *Rules* relationship, then it just may never work out in the end. In any case, the only way to find out is to ask him!

Some women are aghast when we suggest their asking a guy's intentions. They argue, "Isn't that aggressive?" or "Shouldn't love be love?" or "I thought saying that wasn't *The Rules*." Others are simply afraid to find out the answer. But it's fine, really! If you ask and your boyfriend changes the subject, gets irritated, or says that it's a bad time and he can't commit because of work issues or finances, then you might have to tell him that you're old-fashioned and don't believe in dating forever. If he still rattles off excuses, suggest taking a break. Tell him to think about it on his own time and call you when he is ready to commit. *Rules* Girls do not suggest couples counseling; we simply disappear and give him all the space he wants until he misses us enough to propose—or not. The truth is that a guy usually knows in the first few dates if he can see himself marrying you or not; the rest of the relationship is just a lot of details.

On the other hand, if he happily alludes to future plans but doesn't say anything specific, when can you expect him to propose and what should you do until then? Women can go crazy during this waiting period between getting a verbal commitment and getting the ring. They really want to push things along, and have little patience and high tension. Their boyfriends have the power to make them a Mrs. or send them back to Match.com—we get that it's stressful! Our suggestion is to diplomatically ask him what his time frame is. We typically tell clients to say, "I've been enjoying our time together, but was just wondering what your intentions are and what your timetable is like."

If he says, "Don't worry, we'll get engaged soon," then how much time do you give him to wrap it up? We can't tell you how many women have contacted us to say their boyfriend proposed, but without a ring or now won't set a wedding date. It's still all very vague! We tell them to give the guy six months to a year to produce a ring and figure out the logistics. Of course, this time frame may feel like an eternity to a woman who has nothing on her finger, but it's just one more time a *Rules* Girl has to practice restraint! Remember, guys often want to propose in their own way—women must let them. Don't bring up stone cuts, settings, or any ring talk until he asks. If you push too hard, he will feel that you just want the ring or the wedding—not him. But if our suggested yearlong waiting period comes and goes and you still have no ring, you might have to break up with him. *Rules* Girls are not gold diggers, but we are not doormats either.

Alyssa, thirty, contacted us to help get her boyfriend of three years to commit. It was a *Rules* beginning, but she regularly saw him five times a week, accompanied him on six different weeklong vacations, and texted him often; he was in no rush to get married. He kept moving back the date he would propose, from Memorial Day to Labor Day weekend to his birthday and then her birthday. We were obviously skeptical. She stopped seeing him so much for a few weeks so he had a chance to miss her and then nicely told him, "I'm old-fashioned. I don't know if I can see you anymore without a ring and a wedding date." He told her he had commitment issues stemming from his parents' messy divorce and didn't know when he would be ready. He suggested they do couples counseling, but he still wasn't ready, even after eight sessions. We told her, "Next!" After she broke up with him, he quickly e-mailed her to ask where he should send her things and then never contacted her again. She was crushed! It was a painful lesson, and a long one to learn, but Alyssa agreed never to spend so much time with a guy again.

On a happier note, April, thirty-five, who was dating her

boyfriend for two and a half years, now has a ring and a wedding date. Her divorced boyfriend was talking about the future only in general terms. She had asked him many times when they would get married and he said that he couldn't think about it right then because of the economy and "things going on with his ex and two young children." She contacted us because she wanted to know if he was serious or stringing her along. We put her on a three-month plan of seeing him less and not mentioning marriage *at all.* At the end, she gave him the ultimatum: "I've been enjoying our time together, but I'm old-fashioned and can't keep seeing you without being engaged." April could not wait to tell us his response: "If marrying you is the only way I can see you more, let's do it."

The difference between Alyssa's and April's story is *Rules* broken along the way. Regardless, the only way to know if a guy is planning to marry you is to ask his intentions, assuming everything else is good. *Rules* Girls don't waste time! A guy who says he loves you but can't marry you for any reason simply doesn't love you enough. Cut your losses and find someone who *does* see a future with you, no matter what else is going on in his life!

Happily Ever After!

We love happy endings! We constantly get wedding announcements from *Rules* Girls around the world and even have a success stories section on our website. Here's one of our favorite stories, which we heard as we were writing this book. Our client Tracy was in the Swiss Alps pretending to enjoy skiing. Todd, her boyfriend of thirteen months, whisked her away to Switzerland for a four-day weekend to celebrate her thirty-third birthday. Tracy wanted to celebrate with a sparkly diamond ring on her finger—she also hated skiing and had nothing to wear—but we told her to go anyway. She begrudgingly agreed and promised to check in with us on her BlackBerry. Weeks earlier, she had asked his intentions and he said that he didn't like having "a gun put to his head." We told her not to react but to keep in mind that guys will sometimes test you to see if you will let them propose the way they want to—or if you're going to be a difficult diva.

We had been working with Tracy ever since Todd, thirty-eight, reached out to her on Match.com. The pretty brunette party planner had a history of whirlwind courtships that never panned out and was determined to do things differently this time. Tracy was on a strict boot-camp plan—seeing Todd only twice a week, keeping texting to a minimum, and disappearing in between dates. Todd brought up the future in a general way, but made it crystal clear he was in no rush to get married, having been through a messy breakup with his live-in ex-girlfriend of three years.

Tracy's birthday came and went on the first night of the long weekend, but there was no ring in sight—just a romantic dinner. We told Tracy that it would be too predictable for Todd to propose during her birthday dinner, as most guys like to do it their way and surprise the woman of their dreams. The next day was even worse: she fell off the intermediate slope and tore a ligament in her ankle! She texted us from the mountaintop, "I'm on crutches, I can't ski. Can I go home now? He is so not proposing!" We were sorry about her ankle, but told her just to finish out the trip lest he think she was crazy and marriage-obsessed. We assured her that if he didn't propose by the end of the weekend she could say, "I'm old-fashioned and don't believe in dating for more than a year and a half without a ring and wedding date," and then take a break—after all, he was thirty-eight, not twenty-eight!

Two days later we got an e-mail from Tracy saying, "He did it! I'm so happy, details to come!" On the last night of the trip during a romantic dinner at a mountaintop restaurant, Todd said his jacket felt heavy and she responded it was probably because it's leather. He said no, there's something in my pocket that's weighing it down...and pulled out a ring! Tracy, a fast talker from LA, was in such shock that she went into a trance and became speechless. Todd talked on and on about their future and she could barely remember anything. So he proposed *again,* which was funny considering she had been wondering whether he was going to ask her at all! She wrote us, "LOL, after proposing twice he asked me, 'Now will you return all my calls and texts?'" We wrote back, "Sure, whatever he wants...you were hard to get, now be easy to be with!"

Why did we bring all this up? Because Tracy didn't always feel like doing *The Rules* when she was working with us. She sometimes wanted to see Todd five times a week; she would have texted him and texted him back all day; she would have gone on a weeklong trip to Europe with him after knowing him for only three months; and she might have lived with him as well. On her own, she might have screamed, "Skiing????!!! Are you kidding me? Are you going to marry me or not?" or "I can't believe you didn't propose on my birthday!" Without *The Rules*, Tracy would have blown it! But Tracy played hard to get and got her Mr. Right.

Rule #31

Next! and Other *Rules* for Dealing with Rejection

BEING REJECTED IS never easy, no matter how wrong a guy is for you or how much wrong he did you. Today rejection can be even more painful than ever before. A guy can announce the breakup on Facebook or that he's "finally single" on Twitter. He can forward around nasty e-mails and cause you public humiliation in addition to private anguish. And if you do decide to stay connected to your ex on these sites, you may see status updates or photos of him with his new girlfriend or other women and find out that he has moved on.

If a relationship doesn't work out, it's because it just wasn't good for you. But most often when women have just been broken up with, they do not want to hear that the guy they are pining for is not good for them—they just want him back!

When women in this situation contact us for a consultation, we do everything we can to find out if the relationship is salvageable. If we think our client made a mistake that can be fixed or that there is the slightest chance of getting him back, we suggest one call, e-mail, or text for closure. She can send *one* message saying something like "Hi, just wanted to see how you are doing" to see if the guy bites. If it was a *Rules* relationship to begin with and he shows interest in reconnecting, she will go on a strict plan of being hard to get but easy to be with. But if it was not a *Rules* relationship or her ex is already dating someone else, we advise her to move on—and quickly. We say, "Next!"—meaning wipe away a tear, go to a party or club where he is nowhere to be found, and join an online dating site ASAP!

Of course, it's not always that easy to move on, and we completely understand and sympathize. Even if the guy was bad news, she may refuse to see it, or ignores it and still wants him back. Maybe he is her high school sweetheart, maybe he is the guy she lost her virginity to, or maybe he is her fiancé. Even if he said, "I love you, but I'm not in love with you" or "We are just not good together," she may want him back. She just wants to talk about him, the guy who got away, and nothing else. She keeps going over and over everything that happened until the breakup, hoping that she can figure out what went wrong and how to make it work again.

She also has many logistical questions. Should she answer his texts? Nope! Accept a booty call? Absolutely not! Should she still give him his birthday present? We don't think so! Write a closure letter going over the relationship and thanking him for all the good times? Nah! And what should she do with his stuff at her place and how should she tactfully get back her things from his place? Who cares! Get a new flatiron. Just get up, get dressed, and get out! Some will, but others refuse to date again until they see photos of their ex and his new girlfriend on Facebook. Whatever works—every woman has to get it into her soul that the relationship is completely over before she moves on.

Here are some *Rules*-y ways to get over an ex:

- **Start dating ASAP!** Did we say that already? We can't say it enough! The best revenge is getting all dolled up and meeting new guys who, unlike your ex, think you are fabulous! How fast, you might ask? The sooner the better. We mean tonight or tomorrow—not a month or five months from now. Women who have been rejected often say they are "not ready" to date so fast, that they just can't even think about it because they feel so hurt. But this mind-set is a big mistake. You can still have your sad feelings, but have them before and after parties and dates—not *instead* of parties and dates. Being caught up in what went wrong with your ex will actually help you do *The Rules* on a new guy because your heart won't fully be in a new relationship—and that is a good thing! We have heard countless stories of women who met their future husband right after a breakup. Why? Because they were still so emotionally involved with their broken relationship that they didn't pay much attention to the new guy—they were a challenge without even trying to be. Plus, meeting someone new will help dissipate your sadness and anger toward your ex. It works both ways.

- **Do a cleanse!** Make it fun. Invite a friend to your place for the purging. Get rid of everything he gave you. Shred, toss, or burn greeting cards and photos, sell any jewelry, and donate books, DVDs, clothes, and other material items. Delete all his texts and e-mails. Don't turn into Bridget Jones! Removing the things from your world that bring him to mind will help you think about him less. This kind of cleanse will set you up for the fresh start you need and deserve. Melissa Rivers confessed on her show *Joan and Melissa: Joan Knows Best* that she did a major purging after a bad breakup with her boyfriend—she bought a new mattress and towels and threw out the computer where she found the sex sites he was frequenting and e-mails from other women.

- **Remember the bad times, not the good times.** If you are going to think about your ex, think about your last fight and how badly he hurt your feelings. Focus on the lies he told you, how selfish he was, that he didn't get along with your sister, and that he was sometimes just difficult. Every time you feel your heart fill up with memories of a romantic date he took you on or how much fun you had at that baseball game, just let those sour memories back in, too! They are the antidote to the longing you might feel after a breakup.

- **Don't write angry letters, texts, e-mails, Facebook posts, tweets, or anything.** There's a saying, "Hell hath no fury like a woman scorned," and it's true. We know women who have posted angry and mean-spirited things like "You'll be sorry" or "You and your slutty new girlfriend deserve each other" or "I want to rip my heart out but someone already did." Don't be stupid. If you send hateful messages, the same guy who said he loved you once could say you are harassing him and threaten to call the police! Your best move is no contact at all. De-friend, un-follow, delete from contacts—whatever you need to do. At this point, don't worry that such a move will possibly show that you care too much: in these situations how you are perceived doesn't matter—it's still the best idea for everyone. Trying to exact revenge will only prevent you from moving on. If you must vent or release some anger, e-mail your rant to a friend or to your therapist so someone else in the world knows how you feel.

Another great option is to write it out and then hit the delete button. But the last person who should read your diatribe is your ex!

Danielle, thirty-two, sent a handwritten seven-page letter to her ex explaining how much he hurt her. (She avoided e-mailing it to him because she was afraid he would forward it to his friends.) But she never heard from him again. When she ran into him one day at the mall, she asked him what he thought about the letter but he denied ever getting it. Remember the episode of *Friends* in which Rachel writes Ross an eight-page letter about whether they were "on a break"? Ross falls asleep reading it and pretends to agree with what Rachel wrote, so they get back together—but once he *actually* reads it and realizes she spent eight long pages blaming him, they break back up! Don't waste your time! That energy would be better spent writing up your new online dating profile.

- **Don't write status updates about your ex or your heartbreak so that all your girlfriends can rally around you.** Ashley, twenty-four, posted on her Facebook page, "I can't believe I wasted a year on a guy who is so immature." In Greek-chorus fashion, her friends commented, "You go girl. Any guy would be lucky to be with you. His loss!" While sweet, this post only called attention to her less-than-ideal situation. It made her sound angry and pathetic to everyone, including any new cute guys!

- **Don't reach out to your ex's family or friends to try to get them to plead your case.** They probably won't and even if they do, he probably won't listen. His mother, sister, or best friend cannot make him change his mind or love you again.

The good news is that every client who moved on quickly and met and married her Mr. Right also realized in hindsight that the guy she had been pining for was wrong for her. "My husband is so much better for me than my old boyfriend. We have more in common and don't fight," said Briana, thirty-two, a client who initially felt too heartbroken to believe that there could be life after her ex. It's true: rejection is usually a blessing in disguise. So if you have just been broken up with, don't get upset or angry. Get even by meeting someone even better for you!

Chapter IV

Guys' Top 20 Turnoffs...
We Know, We Asked Them!

We POLLED HUNDREDS of guys, including college students, twentysomethings, and men through their fifties. We talked to single guys, boyfriends, and husbands. Many said the same things when asked what has turned them off about women they have dated. As you'll see, all the *Rules* we've discussed will help you combat these turnoffs. If you don't know why the guy you are with is losing interest or you are afraid he wants to break up, it might be something on this list. Fix it before it's too late, or work on it for the next relationship!

Here is our list of the top twenty:

1. **Trying too hard.** Guys like girls who are relaxed and go with the flow.
2. **Multiple tattoos, body piercings, and trashy accessories.**
3. **Deliberately running into him all the time** (i.e., at a bar or party) or showing up uninvited at places she knows he'll be.

4. **Texting or checking her Facebook messages while out on a date.** As one guy put it, "Am I that boring that you need to be on your phone with someone else? How would you feel if I did it?"

5. **Writing on his wall in a possessive way** or writing things that are too personal and could potentially embarrass him.

6. **Criticizing him to or in front of mutual friends.**

7. **Hooking up too soon,** since it can come across as desperate.

8. **Overeating or, conversely, giving guys a daily diary of what she's eating and her caloric intake.** As one guy put it, "I don't care that you were eating meatball pizza all day."

9. **Attempting to stay friends with an ex by communicating with him or finding ways to see him.** "This drives me crazy. How would she like it if I was keeping in touch with my ex? Don't make me into the jealous boyfriend you hate."

10. **Not caring about her appearance.** (Guys care about looks more than you'd like to think!)

11. **Flunking classes or getting fired from jobs.**

12. **Codependence.** "If she needs to rely on me to make her feel complete, she probably has some sort of personality disorder or deficit," said one guy.

13. **Complaining about something she can easily fix or change for herself.** When a girl says, "I haven't been to the gym in months, it's really bad," he wants to say, "Then just go!!!"

14. **Wearing too much makeup,** having excessive plastic surgery, or cutting her hair short.

15. **Making friends with a guy's friends so she can hang out in the same circles as he does.** "I'm not talking about girls who become close to their boyfriend's friends in a normal, healthy way—we all want that. I mean girls who forge friendships with a guy's friends in a pushy way early on in the relationship with the wrong motives to get closer to him. It's aggressive."

16. **Too much interest in material things.** "While I like a girl with taste and style, she also needs to demonstrate some interest beyond bags, shoes, and clothes, like current events, politics, sports, and personal hobbies or interests," said one guy.

17. **Double texting.** Nothing is more irritating to a guy than a girl who doesn't have the class or patience to wait for a reply. If you don't hear back after a few minutes, don't hassle him!

18. **Being too argumentative, critical, negative, or sarcastic.**

19. **Getting embarrassingly drunk.** "It's not cute or sexy."

20. **Comparing the relationship to other relationships** and/ or "never being happy in the moment because she's always worrying about the future," said one guy.

Chapter V

Answers to Frequently Asked Questions about *The Rules*

WE'VE TRIED TO address every conceivable scenario about today's dating world in this book, but here we've pulled the most commonly asked questions we get in our consulting service.

Some of this content has been discussed already, specifically *or* generally. Regardless, this section is meant to be a quick and helpful reference guide for you while you're practicing *The Rules*.

Q: A guy texted me, "Hey wanna hang out sometime?" and I wrote back, "Sure," but never heard from him again. How do I get him to follow through?

A: You don't! If a guy asks about getting together, but never gets specific after you agree to it, he is a time waster. Next! We know women who write back, "Yes, when?" or "Great, I am free Thursday and Friday this week and Wednesday next week," thinking that will get him to commit, but it doesn't. Just write back, "Sure," and whatever will be, will be. Trying to pin a guy down never works long term. He might feel obligated or guilty and agree to meet then, but if you have to push him, then it's not meant to be. Remember, guys text lots of women out of boredom while waiting on line at the bank. Maybe the girl he really likes became available and that's why he never followed up. Accept it and move on!

Q: Some of my friends think *The Rules* are crazy and pressure me to text guys or ask them out. What should I do?

A: You don't need to discuss your dating strategy with these friends. Just change the subject or say you're not using any strategy in particular. You can say, "What rules?" It's hard enough to do *The Rules* with a supportive network. The last thing you need is criticism from or controversy with your BFF! Try to find even just one *Rules*-minded friend, join a support group (see our website, www.therulesbook.com, for *Rules* contacts around the world), or look into *Rules* online forums, blogs, phone meetings, etc. There are *Rules* contacts for teens, twenty-year-olds, baby boomers, and divorced women. It's a good idea to e-mail contacts and discuss your dating behavior so you are accountable and not off on your own. Doing *The Rules* can be lonely if you are the only one of your friends not texting guys all day or hooking up.

Q: The guy I am crazy about found *The Rules* books in my bedroom. What do I do?

A: If he likes you, he won't care. If he asks a lot of questions, just say that you signed up for a seminar or something a long time ago and forgot all about it. Don't worry, if a guy thinks you are pretty, whether you do yoga, knitting, or *The Rules*, he will think it's cute and interesting. We certainly don't suggest volunteering any information about your dating strategies, but if he finds out, so be it. It's so not a deal breaker!

Q: Is it okay to use emoticons? Any guidance on text speak?

A: Emoticons are great for friends, but we suggest rarely using them with guys because they show a lot of interest. Keep it simple: just use a smiley face to say congrats and a frown for "sorry you are sick" and leave it at that.

We support using abbreviations like TTYL or LOL, as these make you seem too busy to write full words and long sentences. You should always write fewer words than he does!

Q: How often should I be logging on to the online dating website I'm using?

A: One or two times a day is plenty, but never on weekends. Online dating should not be your whole life—just part of it! Keep in mind that on some sites, other users can see the last time you logged on. But even if you did log on ten times on one boring day, don't worry about it too much. As long as you are not reaching out to guys first, it's not the worst thing in the world and won't stop a guy from pursuing you—he might even think you're always on because lots of guys are writing to you!

Q: **I've had three dates with a guy and he keeps texting about future dates, but I don't feel anything. Should I keep going out with him or end it?**

A: *The Rules* are *not* about dating a guy you don't like. Dating is not a charity. Just say, "You seem really nice, but I don't feel a spark...Sorry and good luck!" the next time he asks you out. If you think he is really nice, you can fix him up with a friend.

Q: **A guy in my office stares at me and always sits next to me at staff meetings and tells me funny jokes. This has been going on since I started working there three months ago. How do I get him to ask me out?**

A: You can't! Some guys like to look, but that doesn't necessarily mean they're interested. Some have girlfriends or are married but don't wear a ring, and some are just bored. It's a fantasy relationship if a guy doesn't ask you out!

Q: **I've been going to singles events, speed dating, and dating online for the last nine months and have not met anyone I am crazy about. The few guys I do like have not approached me. How much longer do I have to do this whole get-dressed-up-and-go-out thing? It's exhausting and frustrating! How do I get myself to keep going when I have nothing to show for it?**

A: Being single is kind of like being unemployed. You don't stop looking until you are hired—or until you meet Mr. Right. If a client tells us that she is taking a break from going out or is canceling her online dating membership, we ask why. Typically she will say, "I'm not meeting anyone good." We think this response is completely irrational. You won't meet anyone if you stop going out altogether. Just make it part of your routine, rain or shine, that you try to meet available men once or twice a week. Make it like going to the gym twice a week, whether or not you feel like it. If you went to the gym only when you felt like it, you probably would not be in good shape. But most people want to get fit even if they hate going to the gym, right?

Q: When a guy says, "Text me" or "Don't be a stranger" or "Friend me on Facebook," is it okay to contact him?

A: No, it's not. He still has to contact you! Doing any of the above would still be initiating. Guys who make this suggestion either have been spoiled by non-*Rules* Girls in the past or are hoping you will do the legwork to keep the relationship going because they're not interested enough. Don't fall for these lines! Guys also say, "I like it when a woman makes the first move," but they don't usually marry that woman. Don't listen to what men say; watch what they do. Men love a challenge, so be a challenge by ignoring these requests!

Q: Why do guys ask for my number and never call me?

A: He's not interested, but he may have wanted to be polite or end the conversation without hurting your feelings. Sometimes a guy will take your number at a party but meet someone he likes better later on. Some guys collect numbers just for the conquest of it or to brag to his friends, "I got eight numbers last night!" Maybe he plans to use it someday when he is lonely or bored or for a booty call. If a guy has your number and doesn't use it within a week or two, he doesn't like you enough. Don't think about it too much, just move on!

Q: **A new guy who got my number texted me for the first time on Friday at 7 p.m. Can I write back four hours later on Friday at 11 p.m.?**

A: No! Just like there are blackout periods on airline-mile usage, there are blackout periods on communication with guys, specifically Friday 6 p.m. to Sunday 6 p.m. Otherwise, you end up in a texting chatfest with a guy who might be texting five other girls on a Saturday night and wasting your time. Wait until Sunday night and text back, "Hi! Super-busy weekend, just getting back to you..."

Q: **A guy contacted me through an online dating site (or e-mail or Facebook) and said, "Here's my number, you can text me." Should I bother writing back?**

A: First of all, don't be insulted that he is not asking for your number. Maybe other women have spoiled him by texting him first or he thinks you don't want to give out your number for safety reasons. Whatever the reason, just e-mail him back, "Okay great, and here's my number as well..." and then wait for him to contact you. Don't say, "I'm not going to text you first, you have to text me"—we don't tell men our dating strategy.

Q: **You mentioned that we get "one text (or call) for closure." I was dating a guy for two months—we were not exclusive—and he suddenly stopped calling three weeks ago. Can I get in touch with him for closure?**

A: No, not hearing from a guy for three weeks *is* closure. You don't have to find out why or make the breakup any more official. The only time to make "one call for closure" is when a guy ends a committed, exclusive relationship and you later realize that you broke some *Rules* and want him back. In that case, you would just text him, "Hey, how's everything going?" and see if he shows any interest in talking or meeting up. If he does, just act really light and breezy and stop whatever behavior you believe turned him off. If he doesn't want to talk or meet, then move on and don't break *Rules* in your next relationship.

Q: I am madly in love with a guy I have been dating for six months. Is it okay to give him my password to Facebook or my iPhone to show him that we have a good relationship and no secrets? And should I ask him for his password to prove that he loves me?

A: No, it's not *The Rules* in any way to have no boundaries or privacy. Love is not about being an open book, ever. Giving a guy your password is like giving him the key to your diary. In fact, it's often a recipe for disaster because it can lead to a breakup if either of you comes across potentially hurtful messages or texts. Being a *Rules* Girl means being discreet!

Q: Is it okay to contact guys on an online dating website just to say hi and ask them to look at my profile? There are thousands of women out there—the chances of my showing up in a guy's search are really slim. I feel like the only chance I have is to reach out first and then do *The Rules* by waiting for him to ask me out.

A: We understand how you feel, but it is not *The Rules* to contact a guy first for any reason. If your profile doesn't appear in his search, then oh well, it wasn't meant to be. *Any* kind of contacting a guy first on a dating site is making the first move, showing that you like him/ his profile, and thus you will never know if he would have pursued you on his own. It's just like tapping on a guy's shoulder at a party to make sure he notices you because there are so many other women in the room! Part of *The Rules* is trusting in the universe that a guy will find you and that you don't have to make anything happen.

Q: What's a *Rules*-y way to handle video chats?

A: Like with everything else, less is more with video chatting. The first time a guy FaceTimes you, say, "I don't really like it." If he asks why you declined, use one of these excuses: "My Wi-Fi is not working"; "I'm not in the mood"; "This is a bad time"; "Nah, not today"; or "I have my phone on speaker and I'm doing other things." If he tries again, you can accept once for every three times and do it for only ten minutes at a time. If he can see you every time he calls, he will get bored! If a guy insists that you video chat with him, then he's a buyer beware. Any guy who tries to make you feel guilty about it is obnoxious and not for you anyway.

Q: Is asking a guy out *ever* okay?

A: No. If you do need a date for a particular event, such as a wedding, we suggest you invite a platonic friend— not someone you have a crush on. Don't attempt to use these events to launch the love of your life, or you may get hurt if he said yes only for the event, but doesn't feel the same way about you. Also, asking a guy to marry you is completely out of the question. Disregard any leap year folktales that say it's a sign of good luck. *The Rules* trumps any superstition!

Q: A dating blogger suggested I tell guys by the third date that I am marriage-minded and looking for a serious commitment so that I don't waste time with someone just looking for a casual relationship. Do you agree?

A: No, we don't. We think it's premature and crazy not only to put all your cards on the table, but also to grill him so soon. Most guys will find it TMI and run. We think it's better to possibly waste time on a few dates than to scare him away with future talk. When you do *The Rules* by acting light and breezy and ending dates first, a guy who likes you will automatically bring up his intentions. He might drop hints like "You're going to love my mother's lasagna" or "My best friend is getting married in June...Are you around this summer?" A guy's intentions cannot be found out by revealing your hand, but rather by listening for his clues. The same guy who might have been interested will probably change his mind if you ask him point blank where the relationship is going on the third date.

Q: A guy I've been casually hooking up with for the last few weeks just posted a photo on Facebook of himself with two other girls! I'm really upset. Should I confront him?

A: Absolutely not. You should ignore it—or do the same! Change your default photo to one of you and some cute guys, but never let him know how much it bothers you. He may be testing you to see if or how you react, or it might just be an inside joke with those other girls. But don't freak out. Facebook doesn't define you or your relationships. You're not exclusive and he doesn't owe you anything. For you to act jealous and possessive like every other girl might scare him.

Q: **How do you get a guy to pick a day for the date? Sometimes I feel like I have to say when I'm available just to stop the conversation from going around in circles.**

A: Many women ask this question. Invariably when a guy calls or texts to ask them out, they go back and forth so much that the women just want to say, "I'm free Saturday night!" But *The Rules* way is to let him say it no matter how many exchanges it takes, lest you seem too eager. So here's how to handle it: If a guy says, "Hey, want to go out sometime?" you should just say, "Sure, that sounds good." Then when he says, "Okay, when are you free?" you should say, "Well, when did you have in mind?" He might say, "How's tomorrow, Tuesday night for drinks?" Of course, being a *Rules* Girl, you would have to say no to a last-minute date: "So sorry, but I already have plans." He might say, "Then how's Wednesday night?" You have to say, "Actually, work is really crazy this week!" Then he will probably say, "Okay, so how's your weekend?" You say, "The weekend is good," but not any specific date. Then he says, "Okay, how's your Friday night look?" Then unfortunately you have to say, "Actually I may have plans Friday night." Then when he says, "Saturday night," you can finally say, "Sure, Saturday night would be great!" No matter what, don't mention the night of the week—he has to bring it up. Remember, he has to fish and hunt; otherwise it will be too easy and he will get bored.

Q: We went on a couple of dates—it's been going really well. But I have an upcoming business trip and am going to be out of town for a while. How do I keep the flow going so this break doesn't disrupt our relationship? Can I text him when I get back?

A: You don't—and no! A guy keeps the flow going, not you. If you go away on a business trip or vacation, you are gone! If you contact him, it might seem like you are not having any fun on your trip. If he contacts you, you can chat for five to ten minutes before you have to go do something better. Don't text him photos of the beach or the sunrise. Don't buy him a T-shirt, you are so busy! Even if your trip was lousy—you got food poisoning, it rained, the plane was delayed—don't contact him. You should not contact him when you return either. He should be marking down the day you return and nailing you down for a date. Let him meet you at the airport or show up at your door when you arrive. If he wants to, he will figure out how to stay in touch and see you again!

Q: The guy I like asked me a week in advance for a date— more than enough time! I agreed to go, but I didn't hear anything else from him for the rest of the week leading up to it. Can I text him to reconfirm? What if he doesn't give me the specifics (where and when) until that day?

A: No, you cannot reconfirm! You are too busy to even notice that he hasn't given you the details. If he doesn't tell you specifics until the night before or day of, oh well. Just be prepared to go and if he blows you off, have a plan B. Confirming shows way too much interest—and weakness. *Rules* Girls don't need to do it; they are cool and go with the flow. Even if you are the type who confirms everything—plane reservations, manicure appointments, lunch with your BFF or your mother—don't do it with a guy!

Chapter VI

20 *Rules* That Bear Repeating

1. **Don't talk about *The Rules*!** In this sense, *The Rules* are kind of like *Fight Club*. You definitely shouldn't tell any guy you are dating or want to date that you are doing *The Rules* or how they should be dating you in order to comply with them. He has to figure it out himself! Furthermore, you don't need to tell any of your girlfriends about them either if you don't want to. In fact, if you don't think your girlfriends will be helpful, encouraging, and supportive, we don't think you should.

2. **What if you just found out about *The Rules*?** If you've been texting a guy nonstop and just found this book, it's not too late! Don't worry that he'll think you're uninterested or rude if you suddenly cut your interactions down—he'll just think you're busy or out with other guys. Haven't you ever gotten suddenly swamped and had no time to write back to your girlfriends? Pretend that's the case now, even if it's not! Whatever you're doing now, whether it's seeing him too much, going away with him for too long, or responding to

his messages too late, *cut back*. Start doing *The Rules* today—see what happens!

3. ***Rules* for turning a friend into a boyfriend.** If a guy isn't asking you out, he's not romantically interested. But if you want to know for sure, you might mention that you are thinking about putting up a profile on Match.com and see how he reacts. Is he encouraging, or does he try to talk you out of it? You can also start being too busy to text him back or to hang out and see if that makes him miss you and possibly ask you out. If none of these subtle tactics work, you can casually ask him if he likes you as a friend or as more than a friend so you know once and for all! We think it's okay to ask this question for clarity, but if he says he likes you, you still need to do *The Rules* on him after that, even though you are such good friends. If he says he doesn't, you can just move on; there is nothing you can do about becoming his girlfriend if he's not interested in you.

4. ***Rules* for the mature woman.** If you're older or consider yourself "old-school," then some of *The Rules* are probably easy for you to master, like not reaching out to him first and not sleeping with him too soon. Some of them might not even apply, like rarely writing on his wall and video chatting with him only once every three times he asks. But all that this means is that you must work harder on other changes that could be preventing you from meeting Mr. Right. Here are our best tips for a woman divorced, widowed, or who never found her Prince Charming to begin with: Don't stay home with a book, knitting, or your flatscreen! Get out there and socialize, even if you have to go to a singles party alone. Be youthful about your attitude and appearance. Grow

your hair a little longer and wear big hoops, a short skirt, and heels—long hair and hot outfits can shave ten to twenty years off your age. Think positive! You are a CUAO—any man would be lucky to meet you!

5. *Rules* **for same-sex relationships.** The *spirit* of *The Rules* still applies: you should never show all your cards, pursue anyone relentlessly, or erase all boundaries.

6. **How do you compete with all the other *Rules* Girls out there?** You don't! You're looking at dating the wrong way if this thought crosses your mind. *The Rules* aren't about trying to win against other *Rules* Girls or even non-*Rules* Girls. They're about attracting the man right *for you*. You have to put a little faith in it and trust that he'll find you! Worry more about weeding out buyer bewares, and ultimately staying with Mr. Right.

7. **If he doesn't call, text, or otherwise get in touch with you, he's not that interested.** Period! No excuses!

8. **If he's dating others, you should, too.** It's not exclusive until he brings it up and a discussion is had. If he's got a chance to choose someone else over you, don't you want that opportunity as well? We think so!

9. **Avoid certain words and language.** Don't talk about your needs, your long-term plan, or what you deserve. Don't use words like "nurturing," "relationship," "bonding," "commitment," "serious," or anything that reminds you of a wedding. Keep it light—you don't want to scare him off too quickly!

10. **Don't be jealous if his ex-girlfriend texts him or writes on his Facebook wall.** As long as he's not the one initiating contact and making an effort to continue the friendship with her, you have nothing to worry about!

11. **Act as if you have no idea how cool Mr. Cool is.** If a fraternity president, varsity team captain, VIP, or even a celebrity is interested in you, it's best to act like you don't know who he is. Don't gush and say things like "I've heard so much about you!" or "I can't believe you're talking to me!" These reactions will make you sound like a groupie, not like a *Rules* Girl. The trick is to act like he is an average Joe. Remember, he is used to women spoiling him by fawning over him, hanging out with him whenever he asks, and becoming close with his awesome friends. That's why these heartthrobs get bored and move on. *The Rules* still apply! Because these guys can get any girl they want, they want the girl who appears uninterested.

12. **The first and second dates can be on any weeknight, but the third date (and pretty much every date thereafter) should be on a Saturday night.** If he keeps asking you out, but not for the right date, keep turning him down with "Wow, that sounds great, but I already have plans" or "During the week is really crazy" until he gets the hint and asks for Saturday (date night) night. It might take a few exchanges for him to figure it out, but anything is better than accepting a casual during-the-week date or offering up Saturday night to him on a silver platter. Remember, guys love a challenge!

13. **Don't accept a Saturday night date after Wednesday.** This *Rule* is plain and simple and is not to be broken! You want to be with a guy who is thinking about you enough to plan in advance—that's a guy who is ultimately going to want to be exclusive and commit to you. Sure, spontaneity can be very fun, but don't confuse a spontaneous guy with a guy who might just be

bored or might have had another girl cancel on him. Besides, *Rules* Girls lead busy lives; of course you've already made weekend plans by the time Thursday rolls around! If he asks you too late in the week to accept, don't reprimand him. Just say that you wish you were available!

14. **Stay calm if he teases you.** He may text you to hang out on short notice and write back, "Okay, Ms. Popularity" when you tell him you already have plans, or he might say something like "I'll take you away this summer, if we're still dating then…" Guys love teasing, even if they really like you! Don't get paranoid or angry—just ignore him. He probably expects to get a rise out of you, and it's best if you surprise him by doing the exact opposite—don't react!

15. **Don't meet him halfway. If he won't travel to see you, then you just don't see him.** Don't worry about being rude or selfish—the *Rule* is that he should arrange his schedule around you. Tell him you just can't get away. Tell him you're super busy and can meet only near your office or in your neighborhood. You'll actually be doing him a favor by making him excited about seeing you! He'll realize right away that he's going to have to work hard to see you and you aren't just going to fall into his lap like other girls who might have spoiled him in the past.

16. **Stop dating him if he skips your birthday or the holidays.** How a man behaves on these occasions (and other special ones, like when you get a promotion) is a good barometer of how he feels about you. A guy who really likes you won't hesitate to change his plans to be under the mistletoe with you on Christmas or to ensure

that you're his midnight kiss on New Year's Eve. He not only remembers your birthday, he wants to spend it with you and make it special. Such instances are just another time when the guy who likes you will plan in advance. In fact, he might plan something special for no reason at all! Regarding gifts, *Rules* Girls are *not* gold diggers, but we are looking for romance. Jewelry is the most romantic gift of all, but flowers, a stuffed animal, a book of poetry, or a weekend getaway—all these show he cares about you, too. If you once mentioned you like Beyoncé, maybe he'll take you to a concert. He'll have a star named for you. He'll buy you a greeting card and write a love note inside it! It's never about the cost—just the thoughtfulness and meaning behind it. Also take note of how he signs his note. "Love" and "xoxo" are preferable to "best" or "yours truly." And in the end, all you have to do is say thanks! Guys who are crazy about you don't need a special thank-you—it is their pleasure to shower you with love. If he gives you a gift card to the bookstore with a card signed "sincerely" and expects you to gush over it, he may not be the guy for you.

17. **Don't live with a man (or leave your things in his apartment).** We understand that dating today has become much more casual than it was when we first wrote *The Rules*. But we stand firm in believing that you shouldn't move in with a man until you've set a wedding date. Living together is not a trial period for either of you to see how you really feel about the relationship, and it's not a solution that's going to fix your relationship or force him to commit either. He might just be a time waster looking for someone to split the rent!

Besides, how can you play hard to get when you're literally available every moment of every day? You can't!
Furthermore, don't just show up at his place with hair
straighteners and feminine-hygiene products unless he
specifically asks you to and clears out space for you;
otherwise he might feel like you are invading his space.
Not bringing your laptop or phone charger will also
help you end your time with him first because you'll
have to go home to get on with your day!

18. **Don't tell him what to do and don't expect him to
    change or try to change him.** Men like to feel in
    control—the average guy wants to spend his time with
    a girl who makes him feel good or better about him-
    self. He doesn't ever want to feel emasculated or inad-
    equate! Don't push plans, fashion styles, or hobbies
    on him—and don't try to break him of his bad habits.
    Men never *really* change; either accept his annoyances
    and flaws or find someone else.

19. **End a relationship or stop seeing someone you like but
    aren't crazy about.** We think you should go on a couple
    of dates with a guy to ensure that you really know how
    you feel about him. But as soon as you're sure he's not
    for you, you can just tell him that. Say, "I think you're
    great fun, but I just don't feel a spark," or "I'm sorry,
    I don't think we are on the same page." You shouldn't
    keep dating someone you don't want a future with—
    it's not good for either of you, and it's not fair.

20. **Be easy to be with.** *The Rules* are about playing hard
    to get—but once you've got him, they're about being
    easy to be with. Take the energy you put into being a
    mystery, and now put it into being a pleasure. Be kind,
    considerate, and patient. A *Rules* Girl is one who goes

with the flow! That's not to say that you should let him win every disagreement or always get his way; you shouldn't. But take care to think of his side of a situation and he will do the same for you.

Conclusion

Dating Is Discipline!

W HEW! WE KNOW we have thrown a lot of dos and don'ts at you! We have tried to cover every conceivable dating scenario in every technology to show you that you can do *The Rules* regardless of your situation. We know that dating today is harder than ever before—that it's almost impossible to be mysterious and unreachable when everyone is glued to their phones and computers. But we also know that you *can* play hard to get—if you really want to, and if you believe in *The Rules*!

Few women want to believe that the secret to dating is playing hard to get. Like most, we wanted to think that you could do whatever you felt like and still get the guy. We thought, "Who wants to wear a miniskirt and put on lots of makeup and show up at a club or singles party to meet guys but not be able to walk over to and talk to the cute guy? What's the point of showing up and not making anything happen? Who wants to wait for a guy (and not necessarily the cute guy who caught your eye) to talk to you first, or wait for him to get your number and then wait *again* for him to text you and then still *again* to text him back?" So much passivity—so much nothingness! We like action, and *The Rules* are the exact opposite. If *The Rules* are a dance, it would be the slowest dance on earth!

Like so many of you, we were raised to speak up and make things happen—to get good grades, be the president of the club, climb the corporate ladder (or, in our case, hold up our book on national TV)—not be wallflowers. Why couldn't moving and shaking apply to men, too? We didn't like putting ourselves on a "don't initiate" plan. We wanted dating to be whatever we felt like—we wanted to make it happen for ourselves. But we decided to do what we knew in our soul really works. The results speak for themselves: loving husbands, marriages, and children. *The Rules* are a discipline because it's doing what works instead of what you may want to do.

This book has definitely been a labor of love—especially because we wrote it with the help of our two lovely daughters. We hope that everything we have shared with you in this book will help you date with self-esteem, boundaries, and discipline, even as technology continues to evolve!

xoxo

Ellen Fein

Sherrie Schneider

Need More *Rules* Advice?

IF YOU'VE READ this book cover to cover and still have a question or problem, please contact us!

Visit our website www.therulesbook.com, e-mail us at consult@therulesbook.com, call (212) 388-7910, or fax us at (973) 422-0048.

Book a phone or e-mail consultation with Ellen Fein and Sherrie Schneider. One-hour consultations include: dating history; analysis of childhood issues that affect your dating behavior and the type of men you date; advice on where to meet men; how to do *The Rules* in person, online, and in every other technology; how to act on dates; how to get a guy to commit or propose; how to move on if he doesn't; how to do *The Rules* if you are engaged or married, separated or divorced; plus personal shopping and make-over tips.

Sign up for *The Rules* Dating Coach or *Rules* School course. Our intensive twelve-week online course trains you to do *The Rules* better and to help other women do *The Rules*.

We also offer online courses: "Rules for Rebuilding Confidence After a Bad Breakup" and "How to Write a Bestseller."

Order *Rules* seminar CDs and DVDs, *The Rules Dating Journal*, *The Rules* note cards, or a gift certificate for a *Rules* consultation.

Find out about live speaking engagements as well as worldwide *Rules* dating coaches, contacts, and support groups at www.therulesbook.com. Follow us on Facebook and Twitter: www.facebook.com/TheRulesOfficialBook and @TheRulesBooks.